D0002067

THE POPCORN REPORT

DOUBLEDAY
CURRENCY

NEW YORK   LONDON   TORONTO   SYDNEY   AUCKLAND

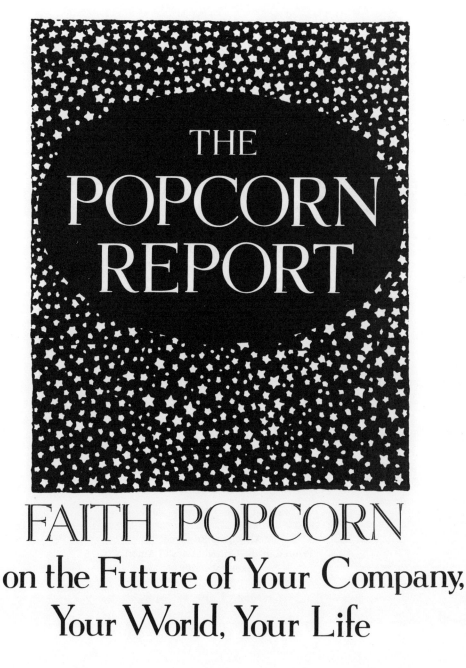

THE
POPCORN
REPORT

FAITH POPCORN
on the Future of Your Company,
Your World, Your Life

A Currency Book

PUBLISHED BY DOUBLEDAY
a division of Bantam Doubleday Dell Publishing Group, Inc.
666 Fifth Avenue, New York, New York 10103

Currency and Doubleday
are trademarks of Doubleday
a division of Bantam Doubleday Dell Publishing Group, Inc.

Library of Congress Cataloging-in-Publication Data
Popcorn, Faith.
The Popcorn report : Faith Popcorn on the future of your
company, your world, your life.
p. cm.
"A Currency book"—T.p. verso.
1. Business forecasting.   2. Consumer behavior—Forecasting.
I. Title.
HD30.27.P66   1991
658.8'342—dc20   90-28832
                                                        CIP

ISBN 0-385-40000-4

This book is dedicated to Lysbeth A. Marigold,
a wise counselor, close collaborator, my best
friend, and the one who created and wrote
tirelessly, endlessly, patiently,
and perfectly.

To Ayse and Robert H. Kenmore, who are
always there for me and finally
"made me do it."

To Rose and Isaac and Clara and George, who
helped shape it and me. Thank you.

Acknowledgments

Special acknowledgment and thanks to Cheryl Merser, who worked on the many drafts of this book and helped very much to form it; to my editor, Harriet Rubin, who guided the vision; to my agent, Binky Urban, an early believer; and to the BrainReserve Family who worked and worked without complaint. Specifically, my love and gratitude to:

Melinda Davis, our very talented Creative Director, whose spectacular ideas are woven throughout; Ash DeLorenzo, Trend Director, whose insight and foresight provide us rich and numerous glimpses of the future; the indefatigable Michele Rodriguez-Cruz, TalentBank Director, who turned herself inside out as usual; Jo-Ann Robotti, our dedicated Director of Projects; Nadja Bacardi, our dauntless Director of Business Development; Debbie Holstein, our wonderful Western Sector Director of Projects; and Carmen Colon-Medina, David Hardcastle, Paul Brennan, Nancy Campbell, Barbara Buckner and Linda Bartsch, all of whom kept the ball rolling; and special, special thanks to Mary Kay Adams Moment,

ACKNOWLEDGMENTS

our TrendView Director, who stayed at my side unfailingly, making sure that nothing went wrong and everything went right; and to my sister and Director of Operations, Mechele Flaum, whose support and unbending belief as always got me through and who watched the "store" while I watched the book.

Many, many thanks to all of the brilliant minds who took precious time out of their already overbooked days and nights to give me their view of the future:

Anthony J. Adams, Vice President, Market Research, Campbell Soup Company
William Agee, Chairman & CEO, Morrison Knudsen Company
Ronald Ahrens, Consumer Group President, Bristol-Myers Squibb
Herbert M. Baum, President, Campbell Soup Company
James R. Behnke, Senior Vice President, Growth & Technology, The Pillsbury Company
Gerti Bierenbroodspot, artist and writer, Amsterdam, The Netherlands
I. M. Booth, President & CEO, Polaroid Corporation
Reginald K. Brack, Chairman, President & CEO, Time Warner Publishing
Jay W. Brown, Chairman & CEO, Continental Baking Company, Inc.
Robin Burns, President & CEO, Estée Lauder USA
Herman Cain, President & CEO, Godfather's Pizza
William I. Campbell, President & CEO, Philip Morris USA
Dr. Marvin J. Cetron, President, Forecasting International, Ltd.
Kenneth I. Chenault, President, Customer Card Group USA, American Express Company
Jay Chiat, Chairman, CEO Worldwide, Chiat/Day/Mojo, Inc., Advertising
Joseph R. Chiesa, Company Group Chairman, Johnson & Johnson
Patrick Choel, Chairman, Elida Gibbs-Fabergé, Paris-France
Ben Cohen, Co-Founder & Chairman, Ben & Jerry's Homemade Inc.
Elizabeth Heller Cohen, Group Director, Marketing, Beech-Nut Nutrition Corporation
Janet Coleman, Associate Editor, Doubleday

ACKNOWLEDGMENTS

Robert Collier, Senior Vice President, Marketing Strategy, Interconti-
nental Hotel Group

Edwin M. Cooperman, President & CEO, TRS North America, American
Express Company

Roger J. Crudington, Vice President, Marketing, Jafra Cosmetics, Inc.,
U.S.A.

Hugh Cullman, Vice Chairman Retired & Consultant, Philip Morris
Companies, Inc.

Mary Cunningham, Executive Director, The Nurturing Network

Laurel Cutler, Vice Chairman, Worldwide Marketing Planning, FCB/
Leber Katz Partners

David S. Daniel, CEO, Evian Waters of France, Inc.

Philip Davis, Director, New Product Development, Anheuser-Busch
Companies

Jerry Della Femina, Chairman, Della Femina, McNamee, Inc.

Karen Dubinsky, Marketing Insights, Inc.

Robert Edmonds, Esq., Edmonds & Beier, P.C.

Phylis M. Esposito, Principal, Artemis Capital Group, Inc.

John B. Evans, Executive Vice President-Development, The News Corporation, Ltd.

Carol Farmer, President, Carol Farmer Associates

David Fink, Esq.

Richard Finn, President, Chesebrough-Pond's USA

Peter J. Flatow, President, Ryan Management Group

Sander A. Flaum, President/CEO, Robert A. Becker, Inc.

M. Suzanne Foley, Vice President, Marketing, Eveready Battery Company

Sharon Fordham, Senior Director, Marketing & New Business, Nabisco
Biscuit Company

George Friedman, Chairman & CEO, Gryphon Development, L.P.

Elaine Garzarelli, Executive Vice President, Director Sector Analysis,
Lehman Brothers

Richard Gillman, Chairman, Bally's Park Place Casino Hotel

Cornelius J. Goeren, Director, New Product Development, The Mennen
Company

H. John Greeniaus, President & CEO, Nabisco Brands, Inc.

Amy Gross, Editor, *Mirabella*

Adam Hanft, President & Creative Director, Slater Hanft Martin,
Inc.

ACKNOWLEDGMENTS

T. George Harris, Founding Editor, *Psychology Today* and *American Health*

Donald D. Hollander, President, Roche Dermatologics, Division of Hoffman-La Roche Inc.

R. L. Hunt

Carole Isenberg, Big Light Films

Laurie S. Kahn, Executive Vice President, Director Broadcast Production, Young & Rubicam New York

John Kapioltas, Chairman of the Board, President & CEO, ITT Sheraton Corporation

Mitchell Kapor, Chairman, On Technology, Inc.

David Kearns, Chairman, Xerox Corporation

Sam Keen, author

Ayse Manyas Kenmore, owner, Krause's Sofa Factory

Robert H. Kenmore, President, Equivest Partners, Inc.

William Lauder, Vice President & General Manager, Origins Natural Resources, Inc.

Peter & Sandra Lawrence

Claire Cosner Leggett

Carl Levine, Senior Vice President, Bloomingdale's

Florence Levitt

Judy Licht, television correspondent

Charles A. Lieppe

Michael K. Lorelli, President, Pepsi-Cola East

Oren Lyons, Chief, Iroquois Tribe

Reuben Mark, Chairman, President & CEO, Colgate-Palmolive Company

Ellen Marram, President & CEO, Nabisco Biscuit Company

Ian Martin, Chairman & CEO, Grand Metropolitan Food Sector

Leo P. McCullagh, Director Brand Diversification, Philip Morris U.S.A.

Jack McDonough, Executive Vice President, International Marketing, Anheuser-Busch Companies

Brian McFarland, President, Personal Care Division, The Gillette Company

Bill McGibbon

Gordon R. McGovern, Retired President, Campbell Soup Company

William McKnight, President & CEO, Nabisco Foods Company

Mike Medevoy, Executive Vice President, Orion Pictures

Ellen Merlo, Vice President Marketing Services, Philip Morris U.S.A.

ACKNOWLEDGMENTS

Sandra Meyer, Senior Officer Corporate Affairs, Citibank N.A.

Grace Mirabella, Publication Director, *Mirabella*

James J. Morgan, Corporate Vice President, Marketing Planning, Philip Morris U.S.A.

Joanne Newbold, Newbold Schkufza Design Associates

Sol M. (Mike) Nissel, Partner, Nissel & Nissel

William Norman, Executive Vice President, National Railroad Passenger Corporation

John R. Opel, Chairman of the Executive Committee, International Business Machines Corporation

Peter M. Palermo, Vice President & General Manager, Consumer Imaging Division, Eastman Kodak Company

Frank P. Perdue, Chairman of the Board, Perdue Farms Inc.

Morris Perlis, President & General Manager, TRS Canada, American Express Company

Peter G. Peterson, Chairman, The Blackstone Group

William G. Pietersen, President, Seagram Beverage Group

Robert M. Phillips, Chairman & CEO, Unilever Personal Products Group USA

Rex Proctor, Vice President & Director, Continental Baking Company

Jack Rehm, President & CEO, Meredith Corporation

C. Duncan Rice, Dean, School of Arts & Science, New York University

Phillip J. Riese, Executive Vice President & General Manager, Personal Card Division, American Express Company

Judi Roaman, President, Confetti & J. Roaman, East Hampton, NY

Anita Roddick, Managing Director, The Body Shop International

Peter Rogers, President & CEO, E. J. Brach Corporation

Michel Roux, President, Carillon Importers, Ltd.

Joseph Sadow, Esq.

Eduardo Sardina, Executive Vice President & COO, Bacardi Imports, Inc.

Robert L. Schwartz, President, Lionhead Transport, Ltd.

John Sculley, Chairman, President & CEO, Apple Computer, Inc.

Arthur Shapiro, Vice President, Group Marketing Director, New Products, The House of Seagram

Robert Sheasby, Vice President Marketing, Chesebrough-Pond's Inc.

Allen Sherman, Vice President, New Product Development, Schenley Industries Inc.

John Signore, President & CEO, Continental Baking Company

ACKNOWLEDGMENTS

Thomas Silberg, Assistant Vice President, Director Health Systems Management, Hoffman-La Roche Inc.

Jacqueline Simon, U.S. Bureau Chief & Associate Editor, *Politique Internationale*

Pierre F. Simon, President, Multicorp, Inc.

Janet Siroto, freelance writer

Anne Slattery, Managing Director Retail Bank, Citibank N.A.

Patrick J. Slattery, Coldwell Banker Residential Real Estate Inc.

William T. Smail, General Manager, Acura Motorcars of South Hills

Richard Socarides, Esq.

Howard Stein, Chairman of the Board & CEO, The Dreyfus Corporation

Sylvia Stein, Consumer Eyes, Inc.

Martha Stewart, Martha Stewart, Inc.

Laura Teller, President, Teller Management Consulting

Jimmu Tenno

Eric Utne, President/Editor-in-Chief, *Utne Reader*

W. Anthony Vernon, Group Product Director, McNeil Consumer Products Company

Marchioness Judith Anne Visich de Visoko

Marquis Visich de Visoko

Scott A. Wallace, Executive Vice President, George A. Hormel & Co.

Larry Weisberg, Senior Vice President, Waring & La Rosa, Inc.

Walter Weissinger, Senior Vice President, New York Life Insurance Company

Dick West, Dean, Leonard N. Stern School of Business, New York University

Leslie H. Wexner, Chairman of the Board, The Limited, Inc.

Jim Williams, owner, Williams Inference Service

Bruce Wood, President, Planters LifeSavers Company

Mort Zuckerman, Chairman & Editor in Chief, *U.S. News & World Report*

And four from the original BrainReserve: my first partner, the creative Stuart Pittman; our first assistant, Virginia Danner; dear Max Reimerdes; and New Business mogul (and charmer), Cheryl Hendrickson-Swanson.

Contents

PART ONE: TIMELINES

Prediction: Socioquake!   3

FlashBack: Lessons of a Life   9

You Have to See the Future to Deal
   with the Present   1 2

PART TWO: PATHS TO THE FUTURE

The Year is 2010: Two Visions: Gloom vs. Hope   1 7

Brailling the Culture   2 1

Tracking the Trends   2 4

Trend 1: Cocooning in a New Decade   2 7

Trend 2: Fantasy Adventure   3 4

Trend 3: Small Indulgences   3 9

Trend 4: Egonomics   4 3

Trend 5: Cashing Out   5 0

Trend 6: Down-Aging   5 6

Trend 7: Staying Alive   6 2

Trend 8: The Vigilante Consumer   6 9

Trend 9: 99 Lives   7 8

Trend 10: S.O.S. (Save Our Society)   8 5

PART THREE: GETTING ON-TREND:
BrainReserve's Trend Techniques and How You Can Use
Them to Bring Your Business into the Future

BrainReserve 101: Consulting in the '90s   9 5

BrainReserve 102: Packaging the Future   9 9

The Trends Lens: Discontinuity Trend Analysis   104

The Universal Screen Test   114

TrendBending   118

The Extremism Exercise   121

Twisting the Familiar   125

CONTENTS

PART FOUR: CAPITALIZING ON THE TRENDS OBSERVATIONS AND APPLICATIONS

Future KnowHow   131
Preventive Business: Your First Line of Defense   133
The 1,000 #: Real Help, Twenty-Four Hours a Day   137
Hot-Branding   140
Ask Not What Your Consumer Can Do for You,
    but What You Can Do for Your Consumer   143
FoodFutures   145
ConsumerSpeak   148
How to Tell ConsumerTime   153

PART FIVE: THE NEW MARKETING FRONTIER

Marketing the Corporate Soul   159
The End of Shopping   164
Truth in Advertising   168
Breaking the Age Barrier   171
Cashing In on the Children's Crusade   174

PART SIX: FUTURE SIGNALS

Trend Signals   179
Making It Big (or Even Bigger) in the '90s   183
FlashForward '90s   186
This Is the First Chapter of My Next Book   189
Glossary   190
BrainReserve Reading List   198

Appendix: How the Future Looks to the Fortune
    500 (and Others)   201
BrainReserve Methodology Flow Chart   213
BrainReserve Client List   215

TIMELINES

The future bears a great resemblance to the past,
only more so.

Prediction: Socioquake!

These are bizarre times.

If you thought it yesterday, if you're thinking it today, you won't think it tomorrow.

Once in a great while, events or innovations electrify the world in a full-swing way that permeates and transforms everyday life. The Industrial Revolution. Wars, plagues. The invention of the car. Television. Or the micro-chip. These are changes you can't see coming.

Another kind of a change is germinating today. It's being inspired, not by one particular happening, but rather by radically shifting assumptions about our past, present, and future. These changes will strike deeper than social shakeups have in the recent American past. This will not be a peripheral movement—made up solely of protesting students or the angry poor, though they'll be a noisy part of it.

The new socioquake will instead transform mainstream America.

America is a consumer culture, and when we change what we buy—and how we buy it—we'll change who we are.

I don't believe in all the talk about the end-of-the-century reassessment. I resist the idea that a specific year or time of year makes us do things. Things happen when they happen. The only reason the millennium is a big deal is because people want it to be.

The millennium won't change anything. *We're* the ones who have to make the choices for change.

For the first time ever in the history of mankind, the wilderness is safer than "civilization."

There are no crack vials in the wilderness, no subway murders, no asbestos, no Scuds.

Increasingly, we'll entrench ourselves in the privacy of the fortress—EveryHome in America. The purpose of the fortress? To make us feel safe. Sophisticated distribution systems will stock and supply the fortresses; the chore of shopping as we know it will be over—shopping has to become theater and diversion. The fortress will be the center of production (we'll work at home), the center of security (we'll make the fortresses intruder-proof), and the center of consumption. Penetrating the increasingly impenetrable fortress will be the primary challenge for marketers and manufacturers in this decade.

For the first time in history, nature is no longer our ally but our enemy.

We are the new endangered species. What we eat has become a political issue. The impulse to get fit has been replaced by the *drive to survive.*

"Natural" had been the food label of choice in the past decade. Now the natural food sources are dubious; who knows what landfill lies below our "organic" greens or how many acres of rain forest our hamburger consumption has destroyed.

Soon we'll want our food grown under controlled conditions in hygienic labs. Clean food producers will wear lab coats, not down-home overalls. All the new controlled clean food will be sold with impeccable credentials: chickens with biographies (where they grew up, what they ate); labeled fish from fish farms (next door to restaurants—a new meaning to Fresh); produce with stickers specifying growing conditions (who's handled it along the way, the rating of the local water source).

Serious food. Survival food. Healing food. We will rebel against the discovery that all along rather than "eating to live" we've been "eating to die."

If at present you're saying "no" to drugs, you'll soon be saying "yes" to a different kind of drugs—ones that regulate your mind, mood, memory.

Foods combined with drugs, "foodaceuticals," will enhance the dynamics of the body and the mind. Foods prescribed in doses, foods to keep you alert and younger. Herbal treatments thousands of years old will fuse with "modern" mainstream medicine to create unprecedented new levels of health and well-being. You'll be able to measure your stress levels and better control them. You'll be buying herbs to cleanse and purify your body. Light therapy and aromatherapy will infuse the fortress with soothing and healing properties.

Up against a deadline, America, along with the rest of the planet, will undergo "Adrenaline Adjusting": a magnification of strength that enables people to do superhuman things.

—The *deadline* is environmental; the earth is depleted beyond the point where it can replenish itself.

—The *deadline* is educational; we're failing to teach our children. Twenty-three percent of the U.S. population is illiterate. And the percentage is growing.

—The *deadline* is sociopolitical; too many government officials don't care; they're just concerned with getting reelected. Ethics—we've screwed up on that too. Now we can read about our role models in the scandal sheets or visit them in jail.

—The *deadline* is economic; our collective debt is unmanageable. The economy couldn't be in worse shape. Remember when the threat of a recession used to set off national fear? Not anymore. Now we're living from one recession to the next, with shorter remissions in between.

Now it takes two incomes for most families to even come close to a middle-class lifestyle—that's an eighty-hour work week per family, at the very least. If there's a national plague, it's fatigue. We're even too tired to watch as much escapist TV as we used to.

And what are we doing with our decreasing leisure time? Sorting garbage. *That's* where the industrial age has cornered us.

We're human beings—and consumers—in retreat. I see people ripping off their subscription labels before throwing their magazines away. Why? No one wants to be identified as the world sinks into oblivion. The 1990 Census was a disaster. No one wanted to be counted. We're wearing shades of gray and black. No one wants to be seen. Market researchers can't find consumers to interview. No one wants to talk. (There's a flip-side, too, as there usually is with human beings.) Desperate as we are to hide, we're equally desperate to assert ourselves as individuals. We're making our retreat in cars with vanity plates.

We don't talk about our jobs, our plans, our future around the watercooler anymore. That would be long-termism, and none of us feels capable of planning very far ahead. We don't look to the future as the place we want to live anymore. One has to feel in control to welcome the long term. We don't.

Adrenaline Adjusting will take place as bad gets worse. The undertone of heaviness and gloom that's prevading everything (I feel it, everyone does) will be followed by acceptance. First, a realization that things *are* as bad as they seem. After that comes anger, directed toward the corporations that have been on a century-long "search-out-resources-and-destroy" mission and toward the government that has been a co-conspirator. And finally, after anger, comes the adrenaline that will give us strength to shape up the future.

We can only stand pessimism for so long.

The lift, when it comes—maybe as early as 1992, will take us to this new phase of the socioquake. You'll see the consumer psyche veer toward hope. You'll feel the mood rise. We'll be buying, yes, but buying carefully with a new awareness that buying is a political act having ramifications all the way up the chain of life. After the lift, conviction will replace caution.

This shakeup, this socioquake, will be consumer-driven, which is why business people will want to get in on the act. Companies will have to realize that you don't sell only what you make. You sell who you are. As in a game of economic musical chairs, many businesses will find themselves without a seat when each round of the music stops. These are the businesses that fail to give tomorrow's consumers what they want.

I know this because it's our business to study how consumers are feeling today and how they'll be feeling tomorrow. We've been predicting consumer behavior for our Fortune 500 clients since 1974, when I started BrainReserve, a marketing consulting firm that specializes in developing new products and services and in revitalizing existing brands for the future consumer. These predictions aren't based on some mystical psychic powers, but on a sound methodology we've developed and refined over the years. It's a methodology anyone can apply to any problem, in any business. It can even be used as a gauge to check if your personal life is "on-trend."

Over the years, many of our predictions have been proven right: the importance of Cocooning (the stay-at-home syndrome); the coming of the Decency Decade (1990s), long before George Bush uttered his prophetic words about kindness and gentleness; and the phenomenon of Cashing Out, where men and women have opted to leave the corporate rat race in search of a better quality of life. Clients who have put money on our predictions about the demand for fresh foods, the popularity of home delivery, the consumer hunger for Mexican as well as "Mom" foods, the rise in the birthrate, the success of four-wheel drives, and the failure of New Coke have turned our interpretations of consumer trends into significant product lines.

And what we're predicting for the future is a consumer revolt that will penetrate every cash register, corporation, and household in America.

The future is a serious business and if your customers reach the future before you, they'll leave you behind. Here are some of the questions we're asking our clients to help them keep a giant leap ahead of their consumers.

*A major financial services company. What changes are needed in the mission of a credit card business for the nineties—when spending has come to a standstill?

*A casino hotel. How do you market the joys of gambling to families with children?

*A bread manufacturer. Can a company change the well-entrenched consumer belief that bread is both fattening and filling? (One way is to convince consumers that certain types of bread will help them live longer, healthier lives.)

*A camera company. What is the future of film in an electronic world that may leave film behind?

*A food packager. How do you fight the growing belief that processed food is poison? We're advising one company to identify the sources of their ingredients. And we suggested they set up a second Board of Directors with mothers and kids who can monitor them on environmental decisions.

*A hamburger chain. As people turn away from eating red meat, how do you prevent them from turning away from you?

For the last ten years, we've been telling our clients about this socioquake that's on the verge of happening. And now, as the signs of the shift begin to appear, it's the strangest feeling—almost like a sense of *déjà vu.* I've never seen any changes as total as these before. This decade will see a full turn from fast-track living to a return to home and self-protection. We'll experience a new morality, new religions, new foods, new science, new medicine, new everything. Everything.

There'll be economic casualties of this decade, but those who see the shakeup coming in time will survive it. This book is meant to help you see—and survive—the cataclysms ahead.

FlashBack:
Lessons of a Life

My parents were attorneys: my father, a criminal lawyer and my mother, a negligence lawyer. They were the perfect left-brain/right-brain combination; my father was intuitive and my mother, all reason—qualities that, when balanced, matter the most in business.

The first five years of my life, we lived in Shanghai, China (my father was then in Army Intelligence). My clearest memories are of riding around in a rickshaw with my amah (nanny) and "grazing" at street food stalls (much to my mother's horror). Because life was so dangerous then (fear of being "shanghai'd"), I was sent off to Sacred Heart Convent day school (much to my Orthodox Jewish grandmother's horror).

When we fled the closing Red Curtain (the last plane out), we moved back to our apartment on Eleventh Street, between First and Second avenues in Manhattan. In the years dominated by the middle-class flight to the suburbs, I was the quintessential city kid. I've since wondered whether being outside the mainstream later helped me view mainstream America with a more objective eye.

Growing up, I spent more time with my maternal grandparents than I did at home. My grandmother had been born in America, while my grandfather had come from Russia (claiming, convincingly, that he'd escaped on a horse). They lived a few blocks away from us, where they owned some tenements. My grandfather's maxim was: If you can't watch it, don't buy it. So I'd sit out with him on Second Avenue in bentwood chairs to help him "watch" their buildings.

And that's where I began to learn about marketing.

He had a haberdashery store and together we would decorate the front windows. Then we'd take our chairs back outside and wait. If too few customers walked by without being hooked by our display, we'd pick up our chairs and go inside again to re-do the window. Repositioning a tie at a jauntier angle or changing the color of a shirt, I learned, could convey a different message.

Meanwhile, my grandmother was upstairs in their apartment above the store, keeping the books. Every noontime, like clockwork, she'd take over running the store from my grandfather and they'd pass one another on the stairs, rarely exchanging a word— a marvelous business shorthand. After lunch, they'd again slip by each other in virtual silence, as they returned to their respective posts. I often think of them when I give my TrendView seminars and mention the trend of Cashing Out: theirs was the perfect Mom-and-Pop business, honest and human-scale, a business that ran so well it transcended language.

It was also my grandmother's job to collect the monthly rents; I'd "help" her with that, too. On the first day of the month, the tenants would drop by to pay their rents—all of eight, twelve, twenty dollars a month. She'd sit at the mahogany table in her dining room, and chat with them in Yiddish, Russian, some German, and Ukrainian.

The business worked. It was personal and hands-on, incorporating family and an occasional friend. There was built-in child care for my sister Mechele and me. Family dinner conversations centered around daily problems and solutions—work was never something that stopped at 5 P.M. We talked about the real estate business, the store, my parents' legal cases. Everybody knew everything, and we all helped out where we could. The objective was deceptively simple: get the work done and appreciate the process.

Years later, when I started to formulate the blueprint for BrainReserve, I structured it instinctively around what I had learned from my family. I began by filling up the ranks of the company with my sister and her friends and my friends. Many of my former colleagues were horrified. If you want to be a marketing consultant, *act* like one, they told me. Give your staff important-sounding titles. Develop a scientific approach (cut-and-dried) to what you're doing. Don't share any information with outsiders. And you must hire some M.B.A.'s.

Instead, I hired my best friend, Lys Marigold, a journalist, who turned out to be a genius at generating Big Ideas, at knowing something about everything, and at translating marketingese into English. She worked with us for ten years, always claiming that she was only there "temporarily," and when she left to spend more time in Europe, we were all devastated. It has turned out fine though—we just fax her in Amsterdam with questions and drag her back into the office whenever she comes home. She came home to work on this book.

My sister, Mechele Flaum, now manages BrainReserve—she runs operations, does strategic planning, and oversees client contentment. Plus, following the family heritage, she's still watching over our grandparents' buildings.

The point is that I never wanted a traditional corporation, with each employee sitting robotically in his or her office. I tried to create a community for thinking . . . for I believe what inspires productivity the most is freedom . . . and freedom begets creativity. Having a free and flexible environment provides a place where people can work together to focus on the future.

You Have to See the Future to Deal with the Present

The future is a collective effort. You can't decide on the future alone, and you especially can't create it alone. The whole foundation of BrainReserve is based on a belief in collaboration.

Years ago, when I was Creative Director at Smith-Greenland Advertising, I had this incredibly simple idea: to gather all the smartest people I could find to solve whatever problem was at hand—something like a braintrust or, as it turned out, a BrainReserve.

When my then-partner, Stuart Pittman, and I started our company in 1974, we put the BrainReserve idea into effect. At first, we were only a mini-staff of three (with our one assistant). But every time we landed an assignment, we'd gather together our "Reserve," composed of the best brains we knew—Shirley Polykoff, Martin Solow, Stan Kovics, Ted Shane, Onofrio Paccione, Bert Newfeld—and we'd problem-solve in the wood-paneled library of our temporary headquarters at The Lotos Club.

These brainstorming sessions worked exactly as I'd imagined they would. Good minds working together to solve problems. The thinking technique—with no politics. Very rapidly, our small "Reserve" crew turned into a computerized TalentBank that now has over two thousand members on tap. (*Spy* magazine, March 1991, called TalentBank "our enormous Rolodex of experts.")

Over the years, though meetings were called to figure out specific subjects, I found that we often got sidetracked to other issues. Film people and doctors, for instance, would get into intense discussions about what was new in compact disc players, microwave ovens, or family planning.

By bringing together people who wouldn't ordinarily exchange ideas (or experts who, in fact, might normally be in competition), we've seen thoughts turn into actions: an environmental expert, early on, explained about how important recycling would be; an architect then began designing built-in recycling bins for New Age kitchens; and certain TalentBank members from the media started informing the public about what would be coming.

These "sidetracks," I realized, were the point. The consumer future doesn't come from thin air, but from a confluence of psycho-socio-demographic-economic factors. Experts from each discipline can glimpse maybe one or two parts of the puzzle of what's coming. Bring those experts together and the pieces fit together. You can feel the energy, the pull, the sequence. The future takes on form.

While our TalentBank is formalized, everybody can create a BrainReserve of their own.

Approach the eight or ten smartest people you know and make them your Kitchen Cabinet, your Life Board. Find people in different worlds—if you're in packaged goods, invite a neighbor who teaches psychology, a cousin who writes about computers. Mix ages, education levels, personalities. Tell them what business problems you're having, the kinds of decisions you're looking for. Have each jot down ten changes they envision in the upcoming decade, then discuss how they think the changes will *happen*. Use our trends as mind stimulators. Brainstorming the future works on all topics of work or life. Don't be afraid to ask, don't be afraid to listen.

Instant TalentBank.

The trouble is that too many of us wake up at night feeling all alone and afraid of what's coming. We'd all be better off facing the future together, collaborating in the light of day. We're all in the future together.

For years, publishers had asked me to write a book about the trends, but I wasn't ready. This time, however, the moment seemed right. Doubleday's Harriet Rubin and I concurred on how the future has become mainstream material—and that there is a tremendous fascination . . . and a tremendous fear of it. I trusted my book in her hands.

Although some business theorists are predicting a terrible apocalypse, I hold a strong belief that the future will be better than the present. I want to show people how to find a way out of the gloom. I want to be the one to introduce the new consumer to the new corporations. And I want to add my voice to a positive collaboration on future action.

THIS SENTENCE IS THE FIRST SENTENCE OF THE REST OF THE BOOK. HOPE.

TWO

PATHS TO THE FUTURE

It's got to get better. Or, worse. Then better.

or

"The Future ain't what it used to be."
                    attributed to Casey Stengel

The Year Is 2010:
Two Visions:
Gloom vs. Hope

Pure logic can lead you down the wrong road: things don't always go from A to B, from bad to worse. Following the trend indicators, it's possible to see that they can go from bad to better to, even, best. Here are two distinct scenarios: Linear Logic vs. Trend Prediction; Gloom vs. Hope.

It's 2010.

Try to open your door and you can't, because there's too much garbage piled up outside. While you once spent about 10% of your salary to buy nonessential items, now it costs about 10% more of your salary to get rid of these nonessentials. You'll know who has money and who doesn't by who gets his or her garbage picked up. The newly rich of 2010 will have made their money not by creating new products, but by making the garbage go away—these are the garbage barons. And the owners of any remaining landfills will have a stranglehold on the community.

Or:

We will adopt a consume/replenish approach to living. Replenish and consume. Consumers and corporations alike will have learned that production and consumption aren't the end of the line. The cycle ends with replenishing, giving back.

It's 2010.

More and more systems are breaking down. The pileup of toxic waste has gotten worse. Every year there's another mid-sized city in America that has to be evacuated.

The air's so bad you're only allowed to drive your car three days a week—which is all you can afford to drive anyway, because filling the tank costs about eighty dollars. Different-colored license plates will tell you on which days it's your turn to drive.

Someone owns the air franchise. Air conditioning is now called air purifying. And it costs a fortune.

Another mogul has bought and regulates the water sources. A long, hot bath is a metered luxury.

Or:

Corporate America as we know it today is over.

All the smartest people have left the mega-companies to start socially and ecologically responsible businesses of their own. Given the choice, consumers are more than willing to buy "correctly."

No one has to drive much anyway. Life feels smaller in scale— we're working at home, involved in the world with networks of friends through the electronic systems that bring in and send out information day and night.

Living within our means and resources, we're slowly healing the planet.

It's 2010. An armed guard picks up your children at school and brings them to your walled community. The streets are an arena of drugs and crime, ruled by those have-not generations who were never educated to participate in the world in any responsible way.

You rarely go outside alone, unless safe passage is guaranteed. Public parks are anarchy. To enjoy the outdoors, you pay to join a private fortified park.

Or:

Life seems to make more sense now. In your new neighborhood, you're surrounded by single and family co-housing units— a loose collective. You'll share goods and services: a communal office with all the latest equipment, state-of-the-art kitchen and entertainment areas, a day care center, medical clinic, and parkland.

There are still problems with drugs, crime, and poverty, but much has been done to alleviate conditions: every corporation does more to help educate, employ, and provide for the disadvantaged. And every individual who volunteers for community work gets a bonus of a tax credit.

It's 2010.

America is now a third-rate power. We never caught up. Everything we were afraid of in 1990 happened.

Or:

America has regained its full strength; it's smart, sound, and fiscally healthy. We've caught up. After the socioquake, old-style management has been replaced by a new participatory way of running businesses. The gap between worker and management has narrowed; we have a new respect for the individual. We've finally reemerged as a country that can make *quality* products well, competing in the world marketplace. We've leveraged our service self. Systems are decentralized, humanized. We're again a leader of innovation.

Culture is back in the hands of the people. Creative talent is flourishing. We've reconciled business with civilization. We finally understand that the archetypal givens—earth, air, water— are the real currency of the future.

Values have done a turnaround.

Happiness used to be part of our birthright. When Thomas Jefferson talked about life, liberty, and the pursuit of happiness, he meant that the more opportunities a society allows us, the happier we'll be. The post-doom value system will offer us the happiness of opportunity.

This is the scenario that will triumph—the healing vision. It's the future that consumers want. We can only tolerate disaster for so long before we hunger for a change in outlook.

Then we change our outlook.

Brailling the Culture

The trouble in corporate America is that too many people with too much power live in a box (their home), then travel the same road every day to another box (their office). They rarely turn on the TV, because they're swamped with paperwork. And they rarely even scan every page of their newspaper, because they're too consumed with yet a third box, their In-box.

If I mention an article that comes from *Vegetarian Times*, most corporate managers smile good-naturedly, as if I'm talking about some way-out cult magazine. They don't realize that more and more average people are actually *reading Vegetarian Times*. And they don't understand the danger of not "seeing" what can be predictive.

This kind of cultural autism is numbing corporate America.

BrainReserve's antidote: to scan today's culture for signs of the future. I think of this as "brailling" the culture, reaching out to touch as many parts of it as possible—to make sense of the whole. Compensating for tunnel vision by developing a different sensitivity, a "feel" for what's going on.

Anticipating a new reality is the beginning of the process of creating it.

Tracking the trends is one of the ways we anticipate new realities and help our clients create them.

At BrainReserve, we track some three hundred newspapers and magazines and, in addition, monitor the top twenty television shows, first-run movies, best-seller books, hit music, and Trend-Track to all types of stores (both in America and abroad) for new products. It's the present culture that points the way ahead.

A new TV show takes off? What audience needs is it satisfying? "The Cosby Show," for example, with its family and home values, appealed to viewers retreating from the sexual revolution and settling into their Cocoons. Later on, Roseanne Barr's earthy show signaled a withdrawal from the diamond-dazzle days of "Dallas" and "Dynasty." She's real, she's tough: a Vigilante wife and mother who doesn't mince words when expressing every consumer's anger.

Check the best-seller list of books, movies, products, at least once a month, asking yourself: Why this? Why now? (No diet books? Are people sick of dieting? Or did Oprah prove that diets don't work?) Switch your radio station from time to time. Once a month pick up a magazine you have never seen. Skip reading your trade publications one week (you'll find out what's in there anyway), and read another industry's trade reports.

Look for the holes. I never stop myself from asking whomever I run into—cabdrivers, people at airports, moviegoers on line—what they think about cars or cookies or computers or whatever we're working on.

The future is out there in the world, and the one place you won't find it is the place where most people look for it. It's not in your office.

Whenever I talk to business groups about the trends we're tracking, the questions afterward are mostly from people speaking as consumers, not as marketers. They always want to know what's going to happen, what to do with their own lives, how to plan for their own future.

And I tell them what I'm telling you here. That Gloom is the short-term, Hope is the longer-term—and the trends and methodology that you'll read about in this book are the bridge that will take you to the longer-term, safely and profitably.

Tracking the Trends

The ten trends that follow are a map to the next decade.

Taken together, they profile the consumers you'll want to attract in the years to come. The trends will tell you how these consumers will be feeling, the impulses that will motivate them to buy one product over another, and the kinds of strategies, products, and services they'll accept—or reject. (You'll also be able to find something personally significant in each of these trends.)

The state of mind of today's consumers—their needs, their fears, and the personalized benefits they're seeking—are more important than age or zip codes or numbers.

For instance, your research may tell you that young urban college grads, earning an average of seventy-five thousand dollars a year, are your "ideal" target market. Fine—but what research omits is that now this particular group of consumers is feeling restless, overburdened, and depressed. What they really long for is to change their jobs, move to the country, and live on fifteen thousand dollars a year. Maybe not so "ideal" for you.

Thinking about consumer moods gives a truer picture than thinking about consumer "types"—psychographics over demographics. By using the *trends* to tap into their moods, you might be able to reach those upscale city-dwellers, after all.

Marketing by TrendTracking will indicate a receptive audience for relief products, anything that will ease the burden, lessen the stress.

Trends are predictive because they start small, then gather momentum. If you can connect the dots between the inception of a trend and the impact it will have on your business, then you can fine-tune your product to fit the trend. As each trend builds and makes its way through the marketplace, it increases its hold on the consumer. And because trends last on average ten years, the momentum of the current trends will propel your business, any business, ahead to the end of the decade or beyond.

Though the trends may shift due to outside events—a gas shortage may keep what we call the Wandering Cocooner at home—the impulse behind the trends presented here won't suddenly change. Each of these trends contains enough energy, enough variety, enough stability, to keep working its way through the market arena.

Bear in mind, however, that each trend is merely one fraction of the whole. Don't veer too far in any one direction with only one trend or another. To make your product or business on-trend, you'll need to understand how the trends work together to define the future.

If the trends seem to contradict each other, it's inevitable. Trends merely reflect the coming consumer moods, and consumers are people—full of contradictions.

At BrainReserve, we call these warring consumer impulses "counter-trends" or flip-sides. For example, you eat carefully and exercise rigorously all week. That's the trend Staying Alive. Then, on Saturday night, you "pig out" with pizza, a quart of ice cream, and chocolate chip cookies. You're feeling, with some defiance and guilt, that after a hard week, you "deserve" it. That's Small

Indulgences. It's important to understand that these two trends work simultaneously as trend/counter-trend (or as we call this particular flip-side, Fitness/Fatness).

Think of the trends in the TrendBank as a kind of database to the consumers' *moods,* a rich source that you can tap into to solve any marketing problem. The ten trends that follow will pull together a dimensionalized portrait of the new turn-of-the-century consumers.

What these trends can do is expand your vision—so you can see more clearly *how* the future is going to feel and look. And *how* your business can profit from this unique perspective of the future.

That's marketing to mood.

That's trending.

Cocooning in a New Decade

We're hunkering down, we're holing up, we're hiding out under the covers . . . we're home.   1986

Now we're cocooning for our lives.   1991

The last gasps of the eighties found Americans huddled in high-tech caves. Cocooning, the trend we first predicted in the late seventies, was in full spin. Everyone was looking for haven at home—drawing their shades, plumping their pillows, clutching their remotes. Hiding. It was a full-scale retreat into the last controllable (or sort of controllable) environment—your own digs. And everybody was digging in. The word Cocooning struck such a collective chord in the American psyche that it entered the national—and the international—vocabulary. (Spotted in the Paris Métro, 1991: an ad for sheets that promised the ultimate in *Le Cocooning.) Atlantic Monthly* magazine puts "cocooning" at the top of the list of words being tracked to enter the lexicon by the editors of the *American Heritage Dictionary*. We defined it, when we named it, as the impulse to go *inside* when it just gets too tough and scary *outside*. To pull a shell of safety around yourself, so you're not at the mercy of a mean, unpredictable

27

world—those harassments and assaults that run the gamut from rude waiters and noise pollution to crack-crime, recession, and AIDS. Cocooning is about insulation and avoidance, peace and protection, coziness and control—a sort of hyper-nesting.

We saw it coming while the party that preceded it was still in full swing. Everywhere on the farther shores of chic (a destination everyone can reach in their consumer imagination), the world was one big nightclub-discorama. Going dancing, throwing parties, eating at new restaurants as a new religion. But we also saw signs that the frenzy was turning in on itself. The phrase "Gimme Shelter!" was taking on a new meaning. People were still going out—almost out of habit—but dreaming about the joys of turning in. Where once people came into the office on Monday mornings full of stories about where they'd been, who they'd seen, what they'd done—now the stories were all about staying home, doing nothing at all. This wasn't about being anti-jet set or reverse hip—it was about reality retreat.

Other early indicators of the Cocooning trend that we had actually predicted were: the skyrocketing of VCR purchases and tape rentals; the making of comfort food for the couch; take-out food in general; and the beginning of a new boom of baby-boom babies. (By 1988, 60% of American homes had a VCR, home-pop microwave popcorn sales were a $300 million business, restaurant sales were woefully down while take-out restaurant sales were up to an astonishing 15% of total food expenditure. In 1990 we saw 4.2 million births, the highest number since the big-boom year of 1960.)

Suddenly the shelter magazines were favoring ever-so-English cottage chintz (Mario Buatta) fantasies, a cushy comfort to replace all that hard-edged glass and chrome. People were buying dogs and more dogs! (In 1988, 52.5 million of us owned pets, an all-time high.) Cocooning turned into a major preoccupation, as record numbers of people remodeled, redecorated, restored, and then watched "This Old House" to relax.

Mail-order sales topped $200 billion in 1990, up from $82.2 billion just ten years before. Phone chat lines, rent-a-cat services, the "Video Fireplace," new wider-cut sit-down jeans, were all telling indicators of trend entrenchment. The Joe Boxer pajama company showed a 500% increase in sales. All of which pointed to a rather cozy, comfy kind of hiding, an almost '50s sense of domesticity—even if working matriarchs had to rush home from the office every day to simulate it.

By 1990, we were a decade into our cocoons. Since most trends last ten years, it might have been expected that Cocooning would veer off into another direction in the late '80s (we'd suffer from collective "cabin fever," we'd streamline our places down to the minimum, and return to the outside world, the new center stage). But there was little evidence that we wanted to disentrench ourselves. Instead, we saw a different turn in consumer behavior.

We were going into emotional as well as physical withdrawal. Our answering machines were screening *all* our calls. (I have friends who schedule phone dates instead of real dates.) Some of us are too overwhelmed or exhausted by the stress of life to bother to return calls at all, even the phone calls of friends we really want to talk to. If anything, the early '90s have brought us into a time of heavy-duty *Burrowing*, digging in deeper, building ourselves a bunker—Cocooning for our lives. The talk is of *increased* crime, AIDS, recession, S&L's, and war. In fact, war news resonates deeply in our heart's idea of home. We talk of "hardened shelters" and "sealed rooms" against attack. Americans are buying gas masks. The fear of terrorism keeps us huddling at home. Leave our cocoons? Forget it. Instead, Cocooning has moved into a newer, darker phase—breaking down into what we are identifying as three new Trend Evolutions: the Armored Cocoon, the Wandering Cocoon and the Socialized Cocoon. Cocooning is no longer exclusively about a place, the home, but about a state of mind—self-preservation.

The Armored Cocoon

One telling indicator: gun ownership among women jumped 53% between 1983 and 1986, to more than 12 million. The number of women who were considering buying a weapon quadrupled. Look for major growth in "paranoia" industries: home security systems, anti-snooping devices, computer watchdog systems linked to private guards and emergency help. Bodyguards to rent by the hour, like temps. Home "warehousing" of supplies, of food, delivered safely in armored trucks, to stock and preserve the cocoon.

But let us note that the Armored Cocoon is more than a place. It's a support group, a private club that keeps out more people than it lets in. It's the organization of neighborhood watches, the mapping of safehouses and safe routes from here to there.

If there's one urgent business lesson marketers will have to learn in this decade—and more on this later—it will be finding new ways to reach the hyper-cocooned consumer. To respond, marketers and retailers must shift the focus away from traditional means of access to the consumer—both physically and emotionally—and into the cocoon. Don't expect consumers to come to you anymore. You'll have to reach them in the cocoon itself.

The Wandering Cocoon

Cocooning is about controlling our environment—and we can't limit our environment to the home (although the huge increase in home-centered businesses certainly gives witness to a successful attempt; by February 1991, 18.3 million people were making money in home-based businesses; 65% of these are women.) We want to feel protected wherever we go. We want a cocoon that travels with us. Problem: it takes too long to get to work, too much scary transition time between one cocoon and another. (Note to businesses: the cocoonier the workplace, the happier and more productive the worker. The Japanese are experimenting with office aromatherapy.) Solution: turn the transportation process into its own kind of mobile cocoon. We are seeing this with the way people use their car time already: they're having more "meals" in their cars, watching plug-in mini-televisions at a red light, conducting business and "life maintenance chores" over the car phone and car fax. The new '91 Lexus has the option of a steering-wheel car phone that automatically turns down the radio volume whenever you get or make a call. Japanese car companies are anticipating the trend, too, with cocoon-away-from-cocoon designs that make car interiors more pleasurable and "livable"—even to the point of including a microwave in the glove compartment. Entire families and other togetherness groups conduct mini-lives in mini-vans and in the latest Voyagers and Winnebagos. Cozier cars will make us reluctant to leave this secondary cocoon. Drive time becomes a protected "escape." (Here's an early indicator of what '90s style is going to be all about: luxury on the inside, plain-brown wrapper on the outside, so threatening "outsiders" can't see it, judge you by it, get jealous about it, hit you over the head for it.) There's a bonanza waiting for the marketer who finds a way to exploit this new cultural shift to *drive-time* Cocooning. (Imagine the amazing possibilities when the "personal plane in every driveway" becomes a reality. Under development since 1956, this new individual commuter-flier will soon be available, and the time has never been righter.) And what about the private van, jitney, or bus service as Cocoon, the train as Cocoon, the commercial aircraft as Cocoon?

Airlines must address this heightened security obsession before it is too late. As we see the changeover in airline ownership from former aviators, who gave us a sense of personal, proprietary, even intimate interest in each aircraft, to venture capitalists, who see the planes as nothing more than a paper property, our sense of unease in flying is doubling and redoubling. "Are these guys cutting corners a real flier wouldn't? Am I going to be okay on this thing?"

Here's where I would start with my recommendation to the airlines:

- Recognize the linkage between the Cocooning impulse and the consumer's new demand for less standardization and more "standards of excellence."
- Show the consumer that real people with a real pride of craftsmanship are responsible for the creation—and maintenance—of this flying Cocoon. How about having each team that built the plane sign their names to it in a show of pride and responsibility? Stickers on each aircraft entrance that show mileage, age of parts, last date of maintenance—personally signed inspection certificates?

- *Armor* us a little—why not a guard on every plane? The cop on the corner in the flying Cocoon.

The Socialized Cocoon

"It's lonely in here. I need some company to help me make it through the night." As much as Cocooning is about getting away from it all, it's also—more and more—about a new way of connecting with other people. Finally—some cheery news about the evolution of Cocooning. We're making it into a new kind of party. Not quite London during the Blitz, but close.

Here's the idea: we're very selectively inviting a new kind of guest into our homes. We're entertaining at home, yes, but not for the usual reasons. It's not so much for social or business advancement, or even extended family events. It has more to do with surrounding yourself with soothing, congenial compatriots. People you feel comfy with to help weather the storm.

It's a phenomenon we're calling "Huddling and Cuddling"— inviting a few close pals, the one sister you like, an old army buddy, in for a cozy evening in the cocoon. Probably *not* your clients or your boss or your suppliers. Nobody you don't like. Everybody (a few at a time) you do like—even if differences in age or lifestyle or social standing or whatever might have kept you from thinking of "socializing" with them before. We have seen it with TV war-watch gatherings at home and regular "meetings" of newly united circles that gather to read books aloud, cook together, play with their kids, or revive the old help-out concept of "barn-raising."

The bolder groups form a human cocoon and go out to neighborhood bars in close-knit packs—hence the name we have given this newly emerging social movement, "Saloning and Salooning." The Socialized Cocoon is in its nascent stages—but watch for the development of real market opportunities here. How about the return of the "Cocktail Hour at Home," a potential big resurgence for liquor manufacturers and others, as people set aside the time between work and home for Cocoon-hopping.

Cocooning is evolving and evolving and evolving. When will it come to an end, or be replaced? When things get as bad inside as they are out. Or when things get better.

Fantasy Adventure

*Send me out into another life. But get me back
for supper.*

"Get me out of here!" seems to be the psychic chorus of the '90s.
We seek stress relief with imaginative desperation—escaping
physically into our cocoons looking for comfort, escaping *emotionally* into our fantasies looking for release. While Fantasy Adventure may appear to come from the braver side of the brain,
both impulses are about the same search for safety. What is Fantasy Adventure exactly? It's vicarious escape through consumerism, catharsis through consumption. It's a momentary, wild-
and-crazy retreat from the world into an exotic flavor, a "foreign"
experience, some product-assisted derring-do of the imagination . . . it's an escapist identification with a hero who's gutsier
than you are, able to get rid of all the bad guys and still get *you*
back home for dinner. It's video rentals and aggressively foreign
cuisines and perfumes named Safari, and mountain bikes you ride
to the mall. It's an out-of-body experience you enjoy from your
favorite chair. It's ever-more-exciting exploits undertaken in the

safest possible ways: for the key to the Fantasy Adventure trend is that the risk-taking is risk-free. You cavort through your favorite exotic . . . or dangerous . . . or wicked . . . or luxurious . . . or mysterious world, confident that you're guaranteed safe return. It's adventure-by-association, secondhand sensation. And for most of our overloaded sensory systems, it's all that we need. It's just what we want. There's enough real danger outside already.

We have been watching this turn from devil-may-care to cautious in pleasure-seeking Americans for a while. Not so long ago, motorcyclists were furious when new laws forced them to wear safety helmets. How dare the law intrude on their right to break their own necks? These days, when I go to the country, I often see postcard-perfect little groups of men, women, and children slowly pedaling bikes down country lanes. How risky an adventure can this outing really be? Yet more and more of these "bikers" are wearing helmets—not because the law applies to them (because it doesn't), but because even *little* risks these days inspire big precautions. It signals a change in consumers' sensibilities. First, we wanted to lessen the risk. Now we want to eliminate it altogether.

Here's a rundown on what Fantasy Adventure has brought to the marketplace. Looming large is the manufactured "adventure" locale. One hotel in Hawaii tempts the beach-weary with reproductions of Venetian canals. A chain of hotels in the Midwest offers adventure one night at a time in "FantaSuites"—your choice of tropical paradise, jungle adventure-hut, Bedouin tent. Anheuser-Busch is building a $300 million theme park of exotic places—the Old West, Polynesia, China—in Madrid, Spain. It isn't that Madrid alone is not a perfectly satisfying adventure— only that the theme park is more controlled. Hyatt Hotels Corporation expects to open some twenty-five fantasy hotels within the next few years. Even shopping malls (like Century City in Los Angeles, California) are taking on the aura of adult amusement parks. (In 1987, 235 million people spent close to $4 billion at the real ones.) Disneyland is now attracting more visitors than the nation's capital. And the trend is global. In addition to their success in Japan, Disney is opening a multilingual land just outside of Paris.

In the active area of adventure, there are 3 million active scuba divers (in the United States alone). Last year, 400,000 (one third of them women) became certified and spent millions on gear. Big Business. But a bigger business of Safe Adventure could be a chain of ScubaAquariums with coral reefs, greenery, and fish indigenous to such different environments as the Caribbean, the Red Sea, and the Great Barrier Reef. Quick escape without the hassle.

Food (that telling indicator) is a bounty of Fantasy Adventure possibilities. While a decade or two ago the American consumer had 65 different kinds of fresh produce to choose from, today she has upward of 250—with the big growth in the area known as exotics: kiwanos, coquitos, and purple potatoes join arugula, bok choy, and finger bananas in the aisles of your local supermarket. Ethnic eating has gone mainstream. Sushi, dim sum, sate, blini, Thai food, and Buffalo steak. Adventurous salsa is the ketchup of the new age. Consumption of fennel seed has grown 255% in ten years.

And what about sex? In an era where even the most innocent-seeming attractions can be fatal, we have made pornography the growth industry of the entertainment business (20% of video rentals are erotic films). Mail-order companies (like the Sexuality Library) deliver X-rated books and films to your home. A new French beer, La Bière Amoreuse, is laced with herbs and spices revered for their aphrodisiac effects. The paraphernalia of passion (mail-order lingerie and more) is seeing a rather astounding success. How much of this is being consumed to enhance sex, and how much to replace it, is, of course, rather hard to determine. My guess is that the "theater" of sex—the movies, books, sexy drinks, sex chat lines—is, in fact, replacing a lot of the riskier sexual adventures we saw in the past.

At the very cutting edge of Fantasy Adventure fashion is Turkish-born Rifat Ozbek, who dresses both Madonna and Princess Diana in his ethnic, exotic, and Orientally inspired designs. But on a day-to-day basis, at home, in the cocoon, we interpret Fantasy Adventure with very American, very outdoorsy hiking boots, lumberjack shirts, fishing jackets, and gear designed for white-water rafting when we're watering the lawn in our own backyard. And take a look at the faces that are selling fashion: the photographer's darling of the '90s is dark of eye, bushy of brow, large of mouth, and almost-ethnic. Revlon's "Unforgettable Women" come from

Somalia and the Soviet Union. Estée Lauder's new star, Paulina Porizkova, is from Czechoslovakia.

Log Cabin Chic is a great escape. Cowboys and Indians and frontier home fashion are big. Many of the best-selling decorating books celebrate a look that transports you to another place altogether: Santa Fe Style, French Style, Italian Style, English Style, Country Living. The Fantasy Adventure Cocoon. Or, the nostalgia escape. If you can transport yourself to the past, you don't have to face the future.

In music, we see the rise of the Gipsy Kings: music from the gypsy caravans of southern France—flamenco fire, Moorish melodies, and a streamlined disco beat. One big-selling album of 1991: Paul Simon's *The Rhythm of the Saints* blends Brazilian rhythms with African guitar riffs. Pop music is clearly going global. We love exotic imports. Jamaican reggae, Cambodian heavy metal, Moroccan hypnotics, Yemenite Jewish fusions. Ofra Haza, raised in Tel Aviv by Yemenite parents, has released over sixteen records, many of which have gone platinum. From the French Antilles, we are swept away by "Zouk" (which means "to party"), dance music that is faster-paced than reggae, melding French, African, and Haitian sounds. And Rap, the '90s folklorists.

What is the lesson for future markets? (Especially important for travel, entertainment, hotels, and food.) Enormously motivating product appeal will come from offering the safe and familiar with an adventurous or exotic twist. Added sensory value—taste, texture, sound, smell, color—makes any product more "sensational." What about the return of Scent-a-Rama movies, with scents pumped into the theater? Or Escapist Rooms where scenes and sounds are projected on the wall; for instance, a trip to Kenya or Paris. A California company is actually proposing that in the future tourists should come to theaters built at the entranceways of America's great national parks and view a film on a giant wraparound screen—without ever stepping foot in the parks themselves. Benefits: No more tiring walks, no more tour buses infringing on nature.

Think of what the true adventure counterpart is to the real-life product experience you are offering the consumer. Do gardeners (already a billion-dollar business) want to think of their plots as land carved out of the jungle, won in a covered-wagon land run, or as a perfect English garden? Do electronic equipment owners secretly think of themselves as Captain Kirk of the Starship *Enterprise?*

The challenge is to offer the safely familiar with an overlay of heart's desire.

For even in the most commonplace of experiences we want to be transported—safely.

Out of our lives.

Small Indulgences

And damned if we don't deserve them.

To get a hook on Small Indulgences, think World War II. Think Hershey bars and nylon stockings. In a war-world of deprivation and bad news, chocolate and great-looking legs could make the difference between making it—emotionally—through the week, or not. Some small material "reward"—some little lift of luxe— is sometimes all it takes to make you happy, albeit momentarily. Sometimes, of course, a moment is all you need.

So why am I calling Small Indulgences an of-the-moment trend, if it's really a universal truth, a basic and timeless human impulse? Because the way we are experiencing this impulse now—and the way we are acting on it—has taken on a whole new dimension. There's a *militancy* about self-indulgence now, a strong sense of entitlement. It's not "Oh, what I would give for a [insert your fantasy here]," it's "I *want* it. I will *have* it. And I *deserve* it." (In a consumer culture—that is, a culture that offers choices beyond survival basics—the motive has never been need, but want. Pushing that motivation beyond *want* to *deserve* is a recent, and powerful, cultural transformer.)

The key, of course, is small. What makes the trend *Small Indulgences*, and not unbridled greed, is a sort of balancing of trade-offs, a psychic cost/benefit analysis. We're looking for an emotional fix—an indulgence of the senses, a little ego expression—without the stress of worrying about the cost, the penalty of *really* overpaying the piper (though overpaying a little bit is part of the indulgence). While a decade ago, consumers were overextending themselves to buy showy luxuries, today we're overextended out. So instead of buying a little red car, we buy a little red chair. We keep the affordable ranch house but dress the beds in all-cotton sheets. We take a mini-cruise instead of a two-week jaunt to Europe (75% of all pleasure trips now last three days or less). A massage instead of a spa trip. A new pool instead of a new house. (Or a lap pool instead of a full-scale, expensive investment.) A great haircut instead of a Giorgio Armani jacket. Lobster at home instead of out at a fancy restaurant.

But it's not just about "gratification substitution"—"I'll take this because I can't have that." It's also about choosing one small category in your life and buying the best you can buy in that arena: going to the best butcher or gourmet food shop (specialty foods are the fastest-growing segment of the nation's sluggish food business), buying Claire Burke potpourri instead of Glade, a Mont Blanc pen instead of a Bic, Godiva instead of Mars. And regular visits to Victoria's Secret . . . and the Secret Garden.

Tap in to this trend, body and soul, and you're giving yourself permission to throw caution (that pesky wet blanket of life) to the wind. Abandon yourself to bad behavior. The indulgence—and the risk—is small. Diet and health concerns are favorite targets. The super-premium (super-fatted and flavored) ice cream phenomenon—Häagen-Dazs, Ben & Jerry's—is pure Small Indulgence. (More than $1 billion in sales in the late '80s, with grocers shoving aside econo-brands to make more room for the rich guys. Häagen-Dazs is experimenting with ice cream cafés in Europe: trend-analysis shows it could be gangbusters here, if the cafés are made comfy, cozy, Cocoony enough: Small Indulgences within a specialized Cocoon.) In 1988, 42% of Americans admitted to ordering dessert more than once a month, up from 17%

the year before. And my personal, who-would-have-believed-it favorite: 1989 saw the introduction of Plugra (almost-French for "fatter"), Hotel Bar's new premium butter that promises *more* butterfat than American standards, more like the "silky farm butters of Europe."

I can see the trend at work in my neighborhood in New York City. A designer shoe boutique closed down, and an accessory store—selling hats, scarves, costume jewelry—opened in its place. Everything in it seems designed to enhance last year's dresses. Great new accessories are quick fixes, Small Indulgences.

A couple of blocks in the other direction, there's a tiny storefront selling only roses, in a dozen varieties, imported cheaply from South America. Brilliant: what was once a great luxury is now a Small Indulgence. But I'm afraid that my neighborhood full-service florist won't last long. Big-ticket-item marketers sometimes blanch when I present this trend, hoping for an early trend demise. But Small Indulgences are here to stay for a good while. The happy news for expensive items is that Small Indulgences are "graded on the curve." They have a totally relative scale. What is a Big Indulgence to some is still a Small Indulgence to someone else. And thinking trend-smart can inspire Big Indulgence-makers to rethink, scale down, make their luxury accessible to a whole new "deserver." (How about, for example, a Mercedes motorbike? Or a Maserati mountain bike? A Rolls-Royce pen?) Here's a big opportunity: even more satisfying than indulging yourself is indulging your children. I'm thinking especially about the new population group we're calling MOBY's (Mommy Older, Baby Younger) and DOBY's (the same, only daddys—often on their second (or third) reproductive round)—heavy-duty consumers with the money and the inclination to indulge their Trophy Kids. Witness the William and Clarissa line of premium-quality toiletries for children, the growth of the stuffed animal market from $255 million to $839 million in wholesale shipments between 1982 and 1987 (probably not all for children), and the introduction of such charming premium products as Bear Bath, a special shampoo for dirty teddy bears.

Crucial to this trend is quality. You can't small-indulge yourself on junk. There's no lasting psychic satisfaction in mere tinsel. Consumers are sophisticated about what price really represents.

Value replaces image. Intrinsic worth replaces name. A top-line Timex can beat out Rolex in this decade.

And here's a developing variant of the trend that I am watching closely—and you should be, too. We're calling it "Indulging at Discount," and it's a direct evolution from the quality-at-any-price undercurrent of Small Indulgences. We have already scaled down the size of our indulgence, to be able to comfortably afford the quality standard we demand. The consumer now seems to be saying, "Gee, that was sensible of me—why don't I take sensibility all the way?" So she is looking for quality-at-the-best-price-she-can-find: Indulging at Discount. This may not seem so startling, until you focus on the classic wisdom of the past that says that about half of the luxury of a luxurious purchase is the experience of acquiring it. The solicitousness of the salesperson, the panache of the place, the "acquisitional aura." Not what the consumer believes the night cream can really do, but that she paid $100 for it. Now she seems to be saying, think how great it would feel if I can find the same thing for $65. Or $25. Or $10! [i.e., the exotic, all-natural, but reasonable items at any of The Body Shops]. We're seeing the discounting of high-ticket items taking off around the country. The indulgence is in the quality and not the dollar splurge and the success of the Price Club, and Cheap Sam's proves it. We're down-scaling our expectations all the way back to the bank.

The question, of course, is, will this down-scaled satisfaction continue to sustain us, to feed our self-esteem in the bleak new days of this new decade? Will a post-modern Hershey bar mentality see us through? (Or more simply put, will this trend last?) The good news for marketers: the worse it gets, the more we need them, these little life-enhancing, get-us-through-the-tough-times lifts. The double good news is, I see an upturn in our time—in our spirits, our culture, our economy. An optimist-driven, renewed belief in the future.

And in that case, our appetite for indulgence, small and otherwise, only gets bigger.

TREND 4

Egonomics

It's the I in what they buy.

The clichés of a culture sometimes tell the deepest truths. The songs we sing can give us away. While some say you can psychoanalyze a generation by the themes of the songs it makes popular, I will go even further. Sometimes you can actually *predict* a psychographic shift through music. It's impossible to imagine earlier generations crooning "I Did It My Way" or "I Gotta Be Me" with the same ego-felt passion that was belted out in the '70s and '80s. I might even go so far as to say there was a direct link from these songs to the behavior of "The Me Decade."

The message is: pay attention to popular culture.

This "Me-ness" is at the very heart of Egonomics. But it's a *nicer* narcissism now. We're not talking about the Masters-of-the-Universe megolomania that we associated with the hot days on Wall Street—but more that everybody just wants a little attention, a little recognition of the *no-one's-quite-like-me* self. It's about individuating, differentiating, customizing. And it's a major force to reckon with in today's marketplace. Egonomics means simply this: there is profit to be reaped in providing for the consumer's need for personalization—whether it be in product concept, product design, "customability," or personal service.

When the first Ford automobiles came rolling off the assembly line—shiny, smooth, and, above all, *all the same*, the world came to see uniformity—mass quantities of uniformity—as the mark of excellence for the modern age. Handmade seemed unbelievably crude in comparison. Now the very reverse is coming to be true. Smooth, shiny, and uniform is often now equated with crude and cheap, especially when compared with the individuality of hand-crafted (or somehow individually crafted) products.

Egonomics can be looked at as the sister of Small Indulgences— the other half of the "I Deserve It" syndrome. Where in Small Indulgences the emphasis is on "Deserve," in Egonomics, the "I" takes center stage. "This is a product, a service, for *me*. It was created for me as a tool for my own self-expression. I am not a number. I am different from my neighbor." Egonomics shifts the emphasis from the manufacturer's priorities to the consumer's. Egonomics is niche marketing in the extreme. Think of each customer as occupying her own niche. The marketer who enables each customer to feel unique will succeed.

Publishing is a great place to start in examining this trend. Look, for example, at the difference between newspapers and magazines. A newspaper is a public object, an impersonal, immediately disposable medium of mass information. Just how impersonal it is, is measured by our willingness to read it very openly in public places, our relative indifference even to having a stranger read over our shoulder on a crowded subway car. Magazines, on the other hand, are totally personal. A read-along stranger is *never* tolerated. Magazines are too much an expression of ourselves, delving into their pages an intimate event. I *am* this magazine, we somehow feel, when we make our selection at the newsstand. Even more personal is the secret subscription that's delivered to our door. So it is no surprise that in an era of Egonomics, we see an extraordinary proliferation of narrow, narrower, narrowest niche-positioning for magazines. Magazines for older, retired readers (here's an interesting insight into just how big a seeming "niche" can be: *Modern Maturity*, the magazine of the AARP, has the largest circulation—22.5 million—of any magazine in America); for cat lovers; for above-the-waist-only body builders; for people who like to grow plants in the basement; for waitresses who work the "graveyard" shift. Called "fanzines," some of these smaller, esoterically targeted publications have startling wide readership bases. Those giants, *Time* and *Newsweek*, have made their own forays into Egonomics: *Time*, with its junk-mail cover story issue of November 26, 1990 personalized each of 4 million subscribers' issues by placing the subscriber's name in a blaze of customized glory on the cover; and *Newsweek*, with its ability to print personalized issues, includes different ads for different types of subscribers, such as the recently moved, or senior citizens. The new *Newsweek* program makes it possible to address subscribers by name, and offer them the addresses of car dealerships near them, retail outlets for the specific products they require, or other appropriately personalized consumer tidbits and tips. *Time* has similar capabilities. Egonomics.

John B. Evans, a genius of Rupert Murdoch's News Corporation, says the future of media is in "pinpoint" specialization. "To survive in an information age," he says, "you must be narrowcast." The wonder is not that you can turn on one of forty-eight TV channels and see an esoteric fly-fishing show on the air, but that you can't yet find a show that devotes itself to how to tie flies for Colorado River fishing in months with an "r" for men who like the color blue. It is not the *size* of the viewer base, but its *loyalty* that will make it valuable to the broadcaster.

If the wave of special interest groups forming now is any indication of just how subdividable we are, the answer is "very." We're bonding together against isolation; in groups that bring us together for reasons from personal to political. Cult religions and assorted fringe groups are up: there are at least 40% more listed religious groups than a decade ago, including the Breatharians in California, who believe we can survive without food or drink, and the Searchers, who hold weekly out-of-body meetings. Dancers for Disarmament, The Benevolent and Loyal Order of Pessimists, and Christian Classic Bikers Association are all real names of legitimate and active American groups. Groups like

Overeaters Anonymous (OA), Women Who Love Too Much, and Adult Children of Alcoholics (ACoA) are so successful they have become mainstream.

Egonomics is also at work when overall products and services address the needs of specific identity groups. Groups based on new "life stages," like the aforementioned MOBY's (Mommy Older, Baby Younger) and DOBY's (their daddies); once Yuppies, now they're PUPPIES (Poor Urban Professionals); and WOOF's (Well-Off Older Folks); latchkey kids; Sandwichers (adults caught between caring for their children and their older parents); SKIP-PIE's (School Kids with Income and Purchasing Power)—and groups based on special interests, like Global Kids (kids with strong feelings about the environment *plus* strong influence over family purchase choices); and New Health Age Adults (consumers who consider their health and the health of the planet top priorities).

Consider Egonomics as it applies to Seventh Avenue, the American center of the fashion business. In an earlier phase, we even called Egonomics "Couture for the Masses," because it's all about giving the consumer the custom design and individuating treatment long associated with haute couture—where each garment is individually constructed, fitted, and refitted. The overlay of all this, of course, is that the resulting garment is also recognizable as the work of a single designer. The wearer becomes a member of an elite *petit monde.* In a time of trouble for American retailers and fashion houses, the startling success of a new venture, DKNY, can clearly be seen in terms of its Egonomics quotient. While the numbers of the wearers of Donna Karan designs are small indeed (lovers of her sensual sophistication pay upward of $1,000 a turn-out), DKNY, her lower-priced line, makes her classic clothing accessible to a much larger group of women. Indeed, the DKNY name that's boldly imprinted across every design signals the better fabric and better cut of her all-American tee-shirts and denim jackets, as compared with the ordinary army-navy variety. A clear example of the "I wear, therefore I am someone who appreciates the best" phenomenon of couture for the masses: Egonomics.

Imagine the possibilities of applying the Egonomics trend

quite literally to fashion. You go into a mall, pick the components you want for a pair of jeans (patch or slit pockets, pocketed or pocketless backs, form-fitting or "paper bag waist," any number of design and fabric options). The compu-tailor measures your body (with lasers, perhaps). An hour later you come back and, for the first time in your life, you have a pair of jeans that are made exactly how you want them, in design and in body-fit.

This concept exists already in sofas, instead of jeans. My close friends, Ayse and Bob Kenmore, own a very successful chain of sofa showrooms in the West called Krause's Sofa Factory where you can choose "this arm," "that back," "this skirt," "that fabric," and custom-design "Your Sofa Your Way." Quickly, inexpensively. Egonomically. They also feature the sweetest mini-sofas ("I Shrunk the Sofa") for little kids or even pampered pets.

Or take Belgian shoes—an arcane item to which that Cashed-Out friend of mine, Lys, is devoted. Reminding me of a skit from the early days of "Saturday Night Live" about a Scotch Tape store ("It's something that everybody needs"), the Manhattan-based Belgian Shoes shop has shelves full of shoes—in primarily one style. These slipper-like shoes come in a choice of dozens of "finishes" (different leathers, colors, fabrics, crests, or trims). The point is that you wear the soft-soled shoes for a week or so until they "custom-fit" your feet; then they're returned for a permanent rubber sole. Nobody buys just one pair. That's interactive marketing, where the consumer participates in getting the fit just right. Belgian shoes on a mass scale would be big business. There's still plenty of room for the couturing of the shoe business.

Or, think about Egonomics and the automobile industry. Why not custom seats for people with bad backs? Custom controls for those with shorter legs or imperfect vision? Why can't we get more personal, say, in color and upholstery? Slipcovers for summer and winter? Cars with custom cargo—one trunk and back seat designed for grocery shoppers, another for gardeners? A super-security model for crime-area dwellers? A comfort-and-safety model for young families with kids—with a radar-controlled emergency button that buzzes the local police (wherever you are) for help.

In Japan, a subsidiary of the electronics giant Matsushita makes custom built-to-your-body bicycles under the Panasonic

name—one-of-a-kind creations made by replacing mass-produc-
tion techniques with flexible manufacturing. It's a system that
puts consumers and their needs at the beginning of the process,
rather than after production, at the end. Personal measurements
are fed into a blueprint-creating computer, to produce the high-
tech instructions that guide each step of the crafting process:
taking a total time of three hours versus ninety minutes for a
mass-produced bike. With big profit margins, proud workers, and
satisfied customers, this customizing mode of manufacturing
makes real marketing sense. Why not more of this? People will
buy for *body-fit*.

The cosmetics industry is taking the first steps to Egonomics,
with custom-blended cosmetics (Prescriptives) for each consumer's skin tone, and create-your-own fragrance kits (Perfumer's
Workshop). But there are more possibilities: cosmetics by age, by
character, by season. People will buy for *personality-fit*. No one
knows this better than Louis Licari of the Licari Color Group,
who shuttles between New York and Los Angeles. He originally
studied applied art, turned his creative talents to hair coloring.
("Think of it as a *personal cosmetic*," said Louis.) Each person
gets treated like an original painting—and looks it. He works with
over 1,000 shades of blond, intermingling them for a real born-
blond look.

And what about entertainment? Right now, a company called
Personics makes it possible to customize audio tapes: just pick
out the songs you want to hear or give as a special-occasion gift.
Love songs for Valentine's Day, birthday songs, songs about Dads
for Father's Day.

There are specially tailored cruises and vacations—tennis,
rock, and baseball camps; library cruises; history-and-literature
tours of foreign places; one-day spa retreats. There are services
that pre-edit cable TV listings according to your pre-specified
preferences. And a television/VCR that can be pre-programmed
to tape just what you're interested in: all sci-fi movies made before
1966 or the tennis finals. But the entertainment field remains
wide open for Egonomics.

Home construction equipment remains one industry that is
stalwartly holding to a belief in the convenience of the supplier
over the consumer. Why are cabinets and cooking ranges all the

same height, when cooks come in all sizes? Why, except for premium lines, aren't stove-tops and refrigerators more customizable? Why are there still so few products for left-handed people? Why? Because these changes seem too troublesome to bother with. Because corporations are still operating for their own priorities and not the consumer's.

People will even want their weather customized. There's a company in the Netherlands that has a technology which gives you the option of tropical summer heat in your bathroom, crisp-as-fall air conditioning in your living room. This suggests the possibility that cars or trains can have different temperatures or that autos can be cooler in the front seat (keeping the driver alert) and warmer in the back (optimal child comfort).

As we approach the year 2000, we're still adapting to technology.

Shouldn't technology, by now, be advanced enough to adapt to us?

Cashing Out

Stop the '90s, I want to get off.

If Fantasy Adventure makes your heart beat faster, then Cashing Out is the trend to slow down your racing heartbeat and revive your weary soul. It's not copping out or dropping out or selling out. It's cashing in the career chips you've been stacking up all these years, and going somewhere else to work at something you want to do, the way you want to do it.

You probably know some fast-track, hard-driver—maybe a Wall Streeter or a corporate executive—who suddenly (it seems) leaves his briefcase in the Out-box and resurfaces, smiling, making goat cheese in Vermont. Or running a small New Hampshire newspaper. Or a dude ranch in Montana. Or an environmental action group ten blocks from his old office. Or a classical guitar lover's newsletter ten steps from his bed.

After a decade of greed, after years of commuting, people are dreaming of renovating old houses, starting hands-on entrepreneurial businesses, or even doing what they've built their careers doing—but on their own time and terms. We are asking ourselves what is real, what is honest, what is quality, what is valued, what is really important. We are trading in the rewards of traditional success in favor of slower pace and quality of life. (In 1983, half the country wanted less emphasis on money in the United States. In 1989, three quarters of the nation felt that way, according to *Research Alert.* In a 1989 *USA Today* poll, 74% of men said they would choose a slower career track for more family time.) In the seventies, we worked to live. In the eighties, we lived to work. Now we simply want to live—long and well. Cashing Out has become the way to do it.

Why now, and not at another time in our history? The first obvious answer is psychic cost/benefit analysis. The pace of life has quickened. The ante has been upped. Traditional corporate success demands extraordinary, exhausting effort. We seem to be saying: "Is all this stress really worth the reward?" "Isn't this life I'm living shortening my life?" And the favorite refrain of our times, "Is this all there is?" Adding to that already powerful exit-motivator is our new lack of trust in the benevolence of big institutions. We don't believe in the essential goodness of our government anymore. We have no faith in "parental corporations," and why should we? They've failed to deliver on the basic premise of the relationship: a promise of security in exchange for loyal nine-to-fiveism. We're being laid off as corporations are bought and sold like Monopoly properties. Our health and other benefits are being cut back. Labor's classic mistrust of management has "trickled up" to management itself. But instead of revolution, we are seeing retreat. Away from the cold, sterile, alienating office and back to the welcoming warmth of the cocoon: the home business. Thanks to today's technology.

Cashing Out to the Cocoon

What drew people away from home to work in the first place were the factories; the workers went to the equipment, like slaves to the machines. Then, when the Industrial Revolution was replaced by the Age of Information, the office took the place of the factory. Workers went to work where the information-processors were: management, office equipment, great files of data. The workplace was the repository of information. With the coming of the Age of the Micro-Chip, however, this is no longer even close to being true. Information has been decentralized. The PC, the modem, the fax, the cellular phone, have all made information instantaneously available anywhere. You can have a great laser printer at home. Every member of the family can have an answering-machine receptionist. So why go to the office?

Today, around 16 million corporate employees work at home, either part- or full-time. Most of this work is done after-hours or with informal arrangements, but 3.4 million corporate workers have formal work-at-home deals with their employers. ("Flex-time" and work-at-home flexibility are becoming the newest corporate perks for valued employees.) Add to this the 10 million or so self-employed Americans who operate their businesses from their home, and you come up with a startling 26-million-person at-home army—nearly 25% of the total American work force! (We have been watching this trend for many years now, first seeing it as a female-led phenomenon and calling it HomeComing. In 1988, more than 70% of the businesses operated at home were run by women. Men are now adding to the work-at-home numbers more and more.)

What about the nay-sayers who insist that "office conviviality" is as important a reason to go to work as salary? That group effort is crucial to progress and success? I would respond that their vision is painfully limited. We are not talking about a simple separation of the worker from the office, but over time, a total transformation of the structure of work. Future teams of workers can still meet for conferences and lunches, or gossip-and-coffee sessions over the telescreen. The corporate headquarters, though smaller, can still exist, to provide offices and conference rooms for team projects; large meeting centers for yearly or twice-yearly company "rallies"; and recreation and retreat centers to encourage corporate spirit. Roving secretaries can supply some day-to-day contact.

In fact, every community could have its own neighborhood office center complete with its own "watercooler," offering large-scale office services and supplies (you'll charge these to your company) in a clublike setting. The corporations will monitor their employees the same way they do now, by measuring their productivity. As for the noncorporate entrepreneurs: small, local businesses will rise up to provide collateral services. Niche businesses will move physically closer to their niche markets. "Hoffices"—home/offices—will be the newest real estate development to cash in on Cashing Out.

Cashing Out to the Country

This is a dream as old as America itself: give me a piece of land to call my own, a little town where everyone knows my name. It's a dream we are dreaming with a new heart-and-gut-felt urgency. More than the romance of the country, it's a promise of safety, of comfort, and of old-fashioned values. Getting away from the masses of strangers in the city, and back to family, friends, and local merchants who recognize you when you come in; who become not just resources, but relationships.

If you can't make a real move, you do the next best thing. Wilderness camping is up—from 8.7 million campers in 1988 to 11.4 million in 1990. Even indoor gardening provides a taste of Cashing Out to the Country—and a growing business in the high-tech '90s. More than 80 million Americans are bird-watching! But the *real* move is to the *real* thing. White-collar hotshots are learning to farm. City couples are opening bed-and-breakfasts. (Despite big upfront investment, managerial hassles, and relatively small financial reward, the number of country inns opening across the country is soaring: nearly 12,000 in 1989, up from roughly 2,000 ten years before.) Two pals from New York moved lock, stock, and barrel to start a country company that makes exclusive European-quality linens. Once a month, a huge 18-wheeler delivers European fabric to their barn; local seamstresses whip up creations that retail for high prices back in the city.

Nearly everyone has a story of a friend who has Country Cashed-Out. Or maybe you've done it yourself. Or dreamed about it. It's about quality of life, good schools and safety for the children, cleaner air, more growing space. In the last decade, money was the only factor that counted. Now these other life-value issues are weighing more heavily on the scale. Time to trade in the BMW (bad service, yuppie image) for a Ford Explorer (made in the U.S.A., simple engine). If we can't Cash Out to the Country, we want to live as if we have.

Vicarious Cashing Out

We want to incorporate small-town values into the lives that still hold us in the cities. We wear flannel shirts and hiking boots and watch "The Victory Garden" on TV. We listen to country music on the radio, square-dance in community centers that never saw the likes of such dancing before, and buy cookbooks devoted to "country cooking." We are going back to church in record numbers. (At one time or another, roughly two thirds of baby boomers dropped out of organized religion. In recent years, more than a third of the dropouts have returned. About 57% of baby boomer Americans—143 million people—now attend church or synagogue.) We join groups like The Slow Food Foundation, dedicated to eating slowly and savoring the moment. For a $55 fee, members in twenty-six countries (ten chapters in the United States alone), receive newsletters and a silver pin of the group's mascot, the snail. We order "gardening clothes" from the Smith & Hawken catalog (a look that will soon replace jogging suits as the number-one fashion in America). We decorate our urban and suburban abodes as if we were homesteaders or English country gentry.

And there's an extraordinary phenomenon we have been tracking in Vicarious Cashing Out: a new kind of American hero has emerged from country wisdom, elevating "aw-shucksism" to mainstream cultural esteem. We saw this first in a new kind of commentary: the down-home chumminess of Garrison Keillor on public radio and the Kansas City plain-talk of Calvin Trillin in *The New Yorker* and in his books. Soon it took off in a popular movement we have been calling "The Folking of America": an assignment of high ethos to the simple values we associate with small-town sense and don't-give-it-to-me-fancy insight.

Witness the enormous success of Robert Fulghum's appearance tours and books, beginning with his best-seller, *All I Really Need to Know I Learned in Kindergarten*, and the almost cult-like following of the soft-spoken and reassuring John Bradshaw who invites world-weary adults to rediscover the child within in his best-seller, *Homecoming*. On TV, we feel a collective kinship to such folksy nice guys as Willard Scott, Charles Osgood, and Charles Kuralt. One high-brow, at-home, literary salon on Park Avenue unanimously chose Mark Twain as author of the season. We definitely want life to be folksy and straightforward; to be plain and explainable. That's a major motive behind Cashing Out.

So who will be left behind in the traditional corporate structure? Who knows? The insecure, maybe, and the meanest. Such a threat to corporate America will probably not make the government happy. They'll say Cashing Out in vast numbers is the surest way for America to go down, because there are no great nations structured economically around small businesses. They will be wrong. Nobody works harder, or happier, or more productively, than people working for themselves. The Cashing Out movement will signal no less than the economic decentralization of America—for the better.

Other generations have abandoned familiar terrains for freedom's sake. We're leaving our lives, metaphorically, for self-control. Escaping from the chaos and uncertainty that many of us feel as puppets of corporate America. There's little *actual* freedom, and not much leisure to look forward to, in the realities of Cashing Out. Entrepreneuralism means harder work and a different kind of uncertainty. But that great Emersonian ideal of self-reliance is the reward. Hard-earned.

Down-Aging

"Gray is O.K." New York Times *1980*

We're challenging the biological demarcations of age, re-drawing the line that separates youth from maturity. 1986

An entire, aging generation is re-becoming one big, goofy kid. 1991

It hit us like a bolt from the blue: in 1986, the first baby boomers turned 40. Then, *USA Today* targeted July 20, 1988, as the day the number of people age 35–59 would begin to surpass those 18–34, for the first time since the 1950s. In 1989, Jackie O. celebrated her sixtieth birthday. None of these events, of course, were unpredictable, or of any great statistical surprise; but the middle-aging of the generation that once vowed, James Dean-like, to die young, couldn't help but make waves. It was (and is) a cultural transformation we have been tracking for some time. Not so much from a demographic point of view—though the numbers alone are staggering. (In 1988, 76 million people were 45 or older—a full 31% of the population, and a percentage that is increasing rapidly. The number of Americans over 65 exceeds the entire population of Canada. Right this minute, the AARP represents a full fifth of American voters.) We examined the change, as always, from a psychographic and behavioral point of view.

What we predicted (and now see) is a reinterpretation of the definition of aging, a kind of de-aging of every tier of society. Cher, in 1991, is 45. All aging in at 40-plus, the Rolling Stones and the Grateful Dead are still rocking . . . and rolling. *People* magazine names Sean Connery "The Sexiest Man Alive." Joan Collins, in her mid to late 50's, and Paul Newman, at over 65, are cast as the sexiest of sex symbols. No one questions that Elizabeth Taylor has Passion at her age. More than 10,000 (and a full 42%) of the runners who finished the 1989 New York Marathon were over 40—56 of them were over 70, and the oldest came in at 91.

We are seeing an increase in the number of first-time brides over thirty—even forty (refuting *Newsweek*'s dire prediction that forty-year-old women had a better chance of being killed by a terrorist than finding a husband). We are seeing, even more impressively, an increase in the number of first-time mothers over forty. Connie Chung's maternal intentions, at 44, made the cover of *People* magazine with the headline, "I want to have a baby."

This refusal to be bound by traditional age limitations is the trend we are calling Down-Aging: redefining *down* what appropriate age-behavior is for your age. A profound new phenomenon in the culture, it's the result of more than an unprecedented concern with health and longevity—and even more than a courage born of numbers (aging baby boomers represent a full third of the population). We see it as a truly collective psychosentimental response, fueled in part by a certain New Age Arrogance.

The same baby-boom bunch that once said, "Don't trust anyone over thirty," now says, with equal militance, "Life begins at forty." Whatever the age of this generation, *that* age is the only age to be. Older is becoming better. We still want to look and feel terrific, in spite of the inevitable changes. Americans spend $2 billion a year on products to ward off aging. 40% of women age 25–43 color their hair, usually to cover gray. Retin-A sales reportedly jumped from $20 million to $60 million in 1990. More than one million Americans had facial plastic surgery in 1988, up 17% in two years.

There are some age changes that are coming to be seen as a

badge of honor. It used to be that a *man's* gray hair was called "distinguished"; a woman's, "dull," "drab," or "old." Today, Barbara Bush gains great distinction from her handsome white coif. Famous beauties are now bragging, not lying, about their ages. I predict, that in the emerging decade, the average woman will be much less anxious about growing older, less disinclined to admit to her age. Character will count. If you're secretly planning a face-lift at fifty, you might want to find a doctor who leaves some lines in. Character lines are signs of experience, and they'll count for a lot in the years ahead.

Add to this New Age Arrogance the well-honed sense of entitlement this generation carries with it (maturing baby boomers are the children of relative peace and prosperity, accustomed to being catered to as demanding consumers), and we can foresee the development of enormous market opportunities.

This new consumer will make no apologies for the changes that come with aging, and will not suffer them lightly. Look for a big growth in product technology that deals with corrective hearing and sight. There will be a new at-home dental-care market that offers bleaching and bonding kits as well as gum-disease prevention. And new products that aid dexterity and increase manual skills.

The skin-care market, with accelerated research in anti-aging technology, will see a new surge in vitality. In the works now: anti-aging creams containing the new sunscreen Photoplex, an advanced formulation that blocks almost all UVB rays (the ones mainly responsible for burning, wrinkling, and skin cancer) and also 70% of UVA (contributing to, among other things, skin sagging). And Nayad, a yeast complex that reportedly stimulates the skin's immune system, to help counteract sun damage, sagging, and wrinkling. Shiseido has a new $29 million Institute for Advanced Skin Research in Tokyo, with the announced goal of achieving a true anti-aging drug for the skin within seven years. Or how about brain boosters? Nimodopine, used to improve blood flow in stroke patients, may boost memory capacity in aging brains. Or Deprenyl, a highly effective anti-depressant, shows promise in treating Alzheimer's Disease. It is being called a "psychoenergizer" (it's popular as a human aphrodisiac in Europe). Preliminary evidence shows Deprenyl could prolong your normal life span by fifteen to twenty years! But why can't drug companies do something as simple as re-making a pill container for the gray market that's easier-to-open, has easier-to-read type?

The first aspect of Down-Aging has to do with redefining-down the idea of age: 40 now is what used to be 30, 50 is now what used to be 40, 65 now is the beginning of the second half of life, not the beginning of the end. But the cutting edge of the trend today—and the really *fun* part—is not so much redefining-down as cutting loose—a sort of "let's see just how low we can go." What age is the most fun? How about being stuck at six! It's the let's-be-kids-again impulse in all of us—a partial denial of the burdens of maturity to return to a simpler time when we all giggled and played. Down-Aging is how you explain Dr. Seuss on the best-seller list, *three* movies in one season in which a kid and an adult switch bodies (including the popular *Big:* Tom Hanks as a pre-adolescent), and all that advertising that tells you how Snickers and Oreos and Frosted Flakes and Kool-Aid connect you back to the kid you have inside. Age Arrogance and sheer numbers are what give us the courage to Down-Age—as well as, quite frankly, a deep-felt need to laugh. We are turning, as often as we can, into big goofy kids. And oh, the release it affords us.

At my birthday dinner in May this year, my sister Mechele's contribution was silly ice-cube-sized rubber faces that you squeeze to fill with water. There we were, all dressed up at one of those uptight trendy restaurants, with rubber faces bobbing in all our drinks. At a certain point, one friend filled up his rubber face with mineral water and squirted his dinner partner—who squirted another, and then another, until we were all firing away. Then, one long squirt accidentally strayed—and sprayed diners at a nearby table. Horrified, our party of ten first stared in shock— then started laughing and couldn't stop. Amazingly enough, so did the squirt victims, then the waiter. It seemed as if none of us had laughed that way for a long, long time. We were Down-Aging. Behaving like big, goony kids.

We're so accustomed to stress and anxiety that there's little room for the laughter. To compensate, to Down-Age, we just compiled one of our most successful TrendPacks (a BrainReserve product, page 102), themed around "Humor," and filled it with some "stupid" laughs: a little black box that "swears"; a pig that "oinks" whenever you open your fridge; the comic Jackie Mason's joke book, and *The Encyclopedia of Bad Taste.*

Our country is in search of a good time. Down-Aging is the bridge by which we—adults of all ages—try to connect the carefree childhoods we remember (or at least the carefree baby-boom childhoods the media says we're *supposed* to remember) to the not-always-fun adulthood we find ourselves in now. We are taking our teddy bears with us into our beds; we buy board games we played as children (Clue and Monopoly) for our own kids (we say); and readily admit to loving Nintendo as much as they do (34% of Nintendo users and 95% of the TV audience of "The Simpsons" are adults). Half of the business in Halloween costumes is now for grown-ups, versus 10% just 10 years ago. The hottest radio format is "Golden Oldies"—the number of stations showcasing Elvis, the Supremes, the Platters, and Lesley Gore has ballooned 20% in one year. There's a direct nostalgia value in all of this, but Down-Aging is more than simple nostalgia. What we are doing is chasing after the promise and hope of childhood. Earlier generations drew a distinct line between the pleasures, pursuits, and purchases that were appropriate for childhood and those that were appropriate for adults. Can you imagine Ward Cleaver, Beaver's father, eating a Popsicle? Adults now are re-drawing the line. We eat ice cream pops if we feel like it, or we'll eat the upscaled version of it, in the form of a Dove Bar.

Adults go on their own to Disney World and F.A.O. Schwarz (or to their own grown-up toy stores, like The Sharper Image). We are placing heavy emphasis on recreation: going to movies more (the over-40 movie audience increased 14% in 1989), and attending special adult fun camps (a jazz camp in Vermont, a "simulated space mission" camp in Alabama). We're spending more money now on recreation than on clothing ($247 billion in 1988). One personal Down-Aging favorite is a book entitled *Cool Tricks! A Grown-Up's Guide to All the Neat Things You Never Learned to Do as a Kid* by John Javna, which teaches you how to "Walk the Dog" with your yo-yo and fold a paper airplane, among other really nifty tricks.

. . .

Like other escapist trends, Down-Aging has its darker side: a consumer fear about the very real threats to a safe and prosperous future. The frightened-child-inside-the-adult can't promise his or her own kids that the world they'll grow up in will be bountiful and hopeful, with viable ways to maintain even the status quo for the next generation. The frightened-child-inside-the-adult can't promise his aging parents that he will be healthy, wealthy, and wise enough to take proper, loving care of them as they grow older and feebler. And the frightened-child-inside-the-adult worries about his own old age. Having enough money for retirement is the number-one financial worry for people aged 35 to 49. There is a fear among baby boomers—totally valid—that there won't be enough Social Security to support them when the time comes. That FDIC is no real protection for their savings in the bank. That the world will be in too much of a mess, and we simply won't have the ability to deal with it. (The face-the-issues response of taking positive action is another trend, coming up later.)

With Down-Aging, we are saying to ourselves, even if it's only for ten or twenty or sixty minutes a day, "If I refuse to grow up all the way, then someone else will have to be the adult. Someone else will have to take care of things. *Real* adults have the control, and since I don't feel I have any, I must not be a real adult. I'm a kid!" This feeling lets you cover your head with a cut-out paper bag, make animal noises, and ignore the trouble . . . it's Down-Aging.

What does it mean to marketers? It means when you think of your new consumer, you have to remember the kid inside that accompanies each grown-up on every shopping trip: adult needs, but a kid's lack of impulse control. Adult wants, but a kid's need to cut up and be carefree. An adult's perception of the world, but an overlay of nostalgia and a longing to be reassured that the world is still a wonderful place in which to live. Opportunity is to be found in almost anything that makes you feel better, makes you laugh, makes you have fun, makes you feel like a kid. The *sure* thing for marketers is this: this generation will grow old with a stylish vengeance, putting in more energy against growing old, and the way growing old makes us feel, than any generation that came before.

And spending more money than ever on doing it.

TREND 7

Staying Alive

Do the right thing and you never have to die.

When we talk about Staying Alive—the trend that represents our hyper-quest for health—we are talking about no less than the new American Dream. Once we were looking for happiness—a search that brought the huddled masses, from all over the world, looking for happiness-sunshine-and-gold on frontier shores. It was all based on a fervent belief that somehow, somewhere, somebody had a chance for a better life.

What's the torch we're following today? An extended search—not only for a better life, but for a better, happier, *longer* life. That somehow, somewhere, somebody has the answer to disease prevention, age prevention, the prevention of death itself—if only we buckle under, find the right expert, do the right thing.

Underlying all of this super-positivism is a negativism like none we've ever experienced before. We have a ferocious confidence in the power of experts, for example—but which expert do we listen to? Underneath it all, we believe *no* expert can really be trusted. We are lapping up new nutritional knowledge daily—opening our minds (not to mention our mouths) to an almost-religious belief in the curative powers of food, of diet. Yet at the same time, we are convinced that the foods we are eating are killing us.

Our apples are poisoned! That nice lean chicken has salmonella! That fish we are eating, instead of fatty steak, spent *its* short life swimming with PCB's, DDT's, and other EPA (Environmental Protection Agency) nightmares—a whole toxic alphabet soup of new things to know about, to worry about, to hurt us. In 1990, a national survey showed that 87% of us fear the pollution of our water supplies could make us sick. Our *water!* Many of us are living with the surreal sensation that our lifelong American diet, beginning with what our mothers fed us as children, has been a prolonged and insidious form of poisoning.

And while we're into exercise as never before, exercise itself is now on the watch-out list. Running too fast, too long, too hard, damages your knees, your shins; plus, strenuous exercise is now considered a dependency, like smoking, or drugs, or "loving too much." Right this minute, on my desk is an issue of *Self* magazine with a warning about the consequences of "Exercise Addiction"—is it a healthy habit, or an unhealthy obsession, it asks.

Disease-dread is a collective phobia in our culture—and we're barraged with information that makes it appear quite well founded. We have our modern Black Plague in AIDS, with all its terror and tragedy. And while we want longevity, we are all quite aware that the longer we live, the more open we are to being undone by one of today's horror killers. "Which of today's terrible swords will be the one that does me in?" we wonder. Emphysema, cancer, heart disease. And we feel more and more that we somehow bring it on ourselves.

What we believe now, at least in our darkest hearts, is that disease is not only the result of some unlucky whim of fate or genetics, but often the result of how we choose to live our lives. How we eat, exercise, control stress . . . where we choose to live, what we choose to do . . . whether or not we have the strength of character to pull ourselves up by the battered bootstraps and practice positive thinking. A common theme among cancer patients is just this: "What did I do wrong?" they wonder. "How did I bring this on myself?"

Add to this a collapsing trust in traditional American medical resources (or what traditional American medicine has come to be) and we begin to feel that each of us is out there alone, lost in a world of expertise, opinion, research, and conflicting advice. New real threats and no real help. It's become a cliché to criticize the American doctor, who never comes to your bedside anymore. But look at what the American doctor is up against! Astronomical malpractice insurance costs, and a litigious environment that forces him to practice defensive medicine. Government agencies and insurance companies that question his decisions at every turn—to the point of determining not only how a patient can be treated, but which patients can be treated at all (even who can be admitted to the hospital, and for how long).

The medical consumer is growing increasingly fed up with medical insurance companies, too—paying in for years and years, with no real confidence that the insurance company will pay out when it's needed, when our very lives are on the line. (Watch for a real consumer revolt on this front: insurance companies are in danger of becoming the new villain. A great opportunity for one to emerge as the "good guy" insurance company.) The supremacy of science—that new world-icon—is being questioned. Our medical research is the most advanced in the world, but how many of us can afford or even have access to advanced treatments? And what about *nature?* Has science separated us too much from our "natural" selves? Isn't there some way of bringing them back together?

All of this adds up to a whole new way of looking at health— at the way we live our lives and the way we face our deaths. The driving force behind Staying Alive is a collective, somewhat reluctant, realization that we've all, in the end, got to take care of ourselves. Nobody else is going to do it. We're each inside our own body alone, and the final responsibility is our own.

Self-health care is the future.

The good news is this: taking back responsibility for ourselves means we're not limited to a single expert's opinion, a single school of thought. We have regained a certain element of control.

We become our own investigators, our own decision-makers, our own experts. We counterpoint the advice of the family doctor with the advice of a homeopathist, a reflexologist, a nutrition adviser. We make trade-offs on the basis of the latest research and advice: one study says women who drink moderately (3 to 9 drinks per week) have fewer heart attacks and strokes, another study says moderate drinking increases risk of breast cancer. *Every* health issue seems to offer up such dire trade-offs. At least, we say, we have gained some control, some ability to choose our own demise.

We are rethinking how we feel about food sourcing. With polluted water and pesticide-contaminated soil—not to mention pesticide-contaminated plants themselves—fresh produce has entered that big "question mark" area once inhabited by processed food alone. Organic foods are no longer fringe-y, they're mainstream. A 1990 Harris Poll found that 19% of respondents bought organic produce for the first time, and 30% had changed their eating habits *in the last year alone*, due to news and concerns about pesticides. One survey said 84% of Americans prefer organic foods over conventionally grown produce. (But less than 1% of American farmland is farmed organically.)

Soon the standard of health and reliability will not be farm-grown, but laboratory-engineered. Produce grown hydroponically in "clinically controlled" conditions. (There is already a supermarket—the Fiesta Mart in Webster, Texas—with a 10,000 square-foot hydroponic garden in its produce section.) Feeding standards for livestock—along with genetic finessing—are already changing the fat-to-lean ratios of beef. Can the genetic engineering of new animal breeds be far behind? We may soon be harvesting most of our fish-for-food, from shrimp, lobster, and crayfish to tilapia, out of water-source-controlled fish farms—the biggest source for cultured catfish already. Look for meat, fish, and poultry tagged with their growing history: where they were raised (including soil and water conditions), what they were fed, how they were treated. Laboratory environments may soon be the only guaranteed pure sources.

Engineered-for-health foods are the future. We are already seeing astonishing modifications: not only the entire reduced-calorie food industry (the diet food and drink business is expected to reach $49.6 billion in 1994), but also great new combinations like fluoridated chocolate milk that reduces tooth decay in children, and no-cholesterol cheese. And what about *totally* engineered foods—like fatless fat (Procter & Gamble's Olestra, NutraSweet's Simplesse). In the works: cholesterol-free eggs, bioengineered vegetables with the same protein quotient as meat (but without fat), naturally caffeine-free coffee beans.

Watch the entire food industry change. Food, prescribed in doses, will be preventive medicine. "Foodaceuticals" will blur the edges between drug therapy and nutrition; daily-dose soups or drinks will give you prescribed doses of anti-oxidant beta-carotenes, or therapeutic doses of anti-disease nutritives, or even mood-enhancers. Mood Food to wake you up, calm you down, give you courage, restore your sense of humor. How about cookies with herbs to ease asthma, desserts with bio-active extracts to cure migraines or depression? In Japan, sales of "vitamin tonics" are surging. There are 100 varieties of tonics in individual 50-ml vials, designed for hard-driving Type A's who don't take time to eat right or exercise. Also, "Goal Drinks," with names like "Hard Work" and "Daily Work," made with such ingredients as oyster essence, vitamin C, glycogen, and ginkgo leaf extract.

And we'll see a customization of our diets—by the day, by the week, according to our mood needs, according to our symptoms. Do family dinners really make nutritional sense when every member of the family has had something different for lunch? The personal nutrition adviser is the big growth area in the service business. ("Eat a cup of string beans and two tablespoons of barley, get a good night's sleep, and call me in the morning.") And the big food companies will have to get involved too, with modular meals and menu-planning assistance available by calling 900 numbers: if you have had such-and-such for breakfast, here are our product options for lunch and dinner to meet your particular health/mood goals. We can deliver them to you in an hour. A personal nutritionist for the masses. Products sold as service.

The liquor industry will turn liquor back into "spirits": a shot of rum for PMS, Scotch for a sprained ankle, brandy for a cold. Old wives' medicinal recipes will work their way back into postmodern mythology. Low-alcohol hard liquor will be big, and ultimately, there will be a kind of drink that's hangover- and addiction-proof, as well as non-performance-impairing. Perfect for a middle-aging America. Psychopharmacist Ronald K. Siegel, in his book *Intoxication: Life in Pursuit of Artificial Paradise*, proposes an all-out effort to invent such a safe, but heavenly, high.

The changes in medical care will be astonishing: the biggest of which, of course, is that the patient will be in charge. (Already, sales of self-diagnostic tests and health-care products for *preventive* medical purposes are expected to increase to $2.2 billion in 1995.) Self-health-care will become not only a reality, but a government-guaranteed right, a part of the new American fiber. "Wellness" programs are becoming increasingly recognized as crucial to the future of corporations, not only because of runaway health-care costs, but also because of employee "entitlement." Quaker Oats gives cash bonuses to employees who stay healthy; Sunbeam started a mandatory prenatal course that has dramatically cut the average maternity cost.

Medical knowledge and alternatives will cross cultures in a way we have never seen before. Homeopathy (curing the ailment with a little bit of the "cause"); reflexology, acupressure, and acupuncture (attention to reflex points, pressure points, and the body's energy "meridians" to cure disease); biofeedback; and holistic medicine will move from the fringes to the mainstream of medicine. Even newer-sounding approaches: aromatherapy and herbology, and the ancient Indian ayurvedic medicine (wherein your *prakriti*, or basic body type, determines the correct holistic approach to your health), will be incorporated into traditional treatments, or stand on their own as preferred courses of action.

New health devices (like the Stress Man, about the size of a Sony Walkman, which sends mild electric impulses to calm the brain) will become as common as popular entertainment devices: a Stress Man on every head, a light-therapy machine in every living room. There's a special doorway that we'll pass through every morning that will monitor our weight, pulse rate, body temperature, blood pressure, and other crucial health indicators. An alarm will sound a warning if your vital signs are off and a health screen will flash the best method of correction.

With new research on the effects of sun and light, we will see entire new industries devoted to protecting us from the dangers of the sun's rays, or deriving more good from the benefits of the light spectrums. Imagine lighting consultants who recommend "light environments" or prescribe "light doses" for every member of the family—tailored to optimize each person's energy, mood, health. Cosmetics as medicine—"cosmeceuticals"—will explode as the real future of the "looking good" business, far beyond the anti-aging skin-care creams of today.

Increasingly, entertainment and travel will be health- and longevity-obsessed. Beyond health spas will be mood spas, universal energy gyms, mind-and-spirit "reunions," including therapeutic cruises that slowly take you to healthy places in an effort to heal your body, touch your soul . . . and bring you back twice-blessed.

More and more, we see the very meaning of life as improving the quality of life itself—and life, of course, begins with our own bodies. We may not yet be ready to admit out loud that our goal is truly to live forever. But we will pay anything to Stay Alive.

TREND 8

The Vigilante Consumer

We're mad as hell and we're not going to buy it
anymore!

It's an action-adventure story that strikes terror in the hearts of corporations everywhere (or should). Our heroine, the once timid and trusting Tillie Consumer, changes her name to Attila and strikes out at evil in supermarkets and the marketing world everywhere: attacking trickery, hype, and sham with all the weapons she has at hand: her telephone, her typewriter, her increasingly powerful pocketbook. Try to remember when you might have found this scenario funny. It's not funny anymore. The consumer is fighting back. Tillie-cum-Attila, the consumer, is you and me.

We saw this trend approaching a million consumer-miles away. It was inevitable: the Protest Generation comes of age as the Generation of Super-Consumers. Confronted every day with shabby quality, irresponsibility, and false claims, consumers take up the banner of protest against "marketing immorality." It is social injustice too close to home, and it spawns the next generation of protesters: the Vigilante Consumer.

69

The movement has its own movie-star spokesperson in Meryl Streep, who holds press conferences to alert mothers everywhere about the dangers of alar-treated apples. (Within weeks, *Newsweek*'s cover story asks the question, "How Safe Is Our Food?" and quotes the National Resources Defense Council's terrifying prediction that some 6,000 American pre-schoolers might eventually get cancer from ingesting chemical residues on U.S. products, particularly from apples treated with Alar. Consumer pressure forces an Alar ban.)

It has its modern mythology, latter-day David and Goliath stories, in such individual protesters as Terry Rakolta, an "ordinary housewife" turned one-woman crusader, who single-handedly (with a single letter!) persuaded four major corporations to pull advertising from the television sit-com "Married . . . With Children." Her charge: American companies were profiting from (and promoting) bad taste by supporting what she, and presumably others, considered inappropriate for family-viewing subject matter.

Another crusader is Phil Sokoloff, who led the outcry against tropical oils in cereals and cookies. (Tropical oils, though vegetable-derived, contain saturated fats, and are as cholesterol-elevating, many believe, as animal products.) Whether it was a direct result or not, major manufacturers have, virtually without exception, removed tropical oils from their products. American consumers can now buy their favorite sweets, a bit healthier, from Keebler, General Mills, Ralston Purina, Borden, Pillsbury, Quaker Oats, Pepperidge Farm, Kellogg, and Sunshine Biscuits—much to the manufacturers' (and consumers') credits.

And the movement has its amazing come-back stories: Ralph Nader, after having left the public's top-of-mind for a while (though never leaving the fight), reappears with renewed vigor to speak the people's piece about the high cost of home and automobile insurance. The Sierra Club has also seen a resurgence: it's very vocal against environmental violators, and its membership rolls are swelling.

The Vigilante Consumer trend has even spawned its own brand of television programming. An early show, "Fight Back!" focused on advertising claims. The host/consumer advocate David Horowitz puts products through the same demonstrations that advertisers show in their commercials. Horowitz and his staff have dropped luggage from great heights; had a hard-hat construction worker hang by one drop of glue suspended from a building's I beam; cleaned ovens to see if the single sponge sweep could easily be duplicated; tested the hefty strength of garbage bags and water-soaked paper towels—all the while striking terror in the hearts of demo-devising advertising agencies and clients all over the country. Horowitz congratulates the companies whose claims hold up, calls on the carpet those whose claims don't.

In New York City, CBS's flagship station airs "Shame on You," a news segment dedicated to consumer vengeance. Says chief correspondent Arnold Diaz (quoted in *The Wall Street Journal*): "I want to publicly humiliate people who are doing horrible things." His targets (chosen from the 200-a-day calls to the "Shame on You" hot line): everything from supermarkets that sell outdated meat to real estate scams that strip elderly couples of their life's savings. Victims get to wag their fingers on the air over a rendition of the show's punishing refrain, "Shame Shame Shame Shame on You." It's a highly successful format for news shows all over the country: "Herb's Dump" on KIRO in Seattle, "Shame on You" on WCIX in Miami. Time Warner Inc. is planning a daily show, "Getting Even." Phil Donahue and Oprah Winfrey continue to get fired up over consumer-advocate stories. It all adds up to a powerful hue and cry, a long way from the days when Betty Furness was a lone consumer advocate voice in the television wilderness.

We first started tracking this new consumer behavior in the late '70s and early '80s—before it became a truly militant issue. In those days, the issue was basic product quality. We saw a change in buying behavior: to buying less, but buying better, often guided by such bibles as *Consumer Reports*. We started shopping a little more "defensively"—learning to trade off flash and novelty for more lasting value: the buzzwords were reliability, durability, easy maintenance, ease of use.

Consumers became their own product investigators, researching product quality before they made their choice. (These were the days that turned us all into label-deciphering demons.) After a few years, this work-intensive consuming began to breed resentment. "Why can't *every* product I buy be as good as they say?" "Why do I have to constantly keep my consumer *guard* up?" Add to this growing resentment, a few landmark revelations: The Nestlé company was accused of causing infant malnutrition (even death) because of the powdered baby food formula it had marketed to third world countries. Deadly pesticides were found on table grapes. Children's toys caused fatal injuries. Red Dye No. 2 was found to induce cancer in rats. Consumers were—justifiably—fighting mad. ("Hey, they really *are* out to get me!") They were looking for product quality and uncovering what looked like product deceit. The crux of the issue went beyond quality to ethics: a collective consumer voice began crying out to American companies: "Hey you! Don't lie! Don't cheat! Don't steal!" Our patience wore thin. Our anger became combative. "We're no dummies!" we said en masse. "You can't get away with that anymore!"

For its pure power of expression, my favorite example of this Vigilante Consumer impulse now is the uproar you hear in movie theaters in the Hamptons, when a pre-feature commercial begins to roll. Friends report the same brouhaha all over the country. In Durham, North Carolina. In Independence, Missouri. In Seattle, Washington. In Houston, Texas. "We won't sit still for this!" we seem to be saying. And look at the results in the American marketplace as this militancy focuses on more and more targets. What has the Vigilante Consumer wrought?

Over 200 consumer boycotts: and you can read all about them in the *National Boycott News*, "an independent national magazine for socially concerned consumers," published by the Institute for Consumer Responsibility. Editor Todd Putnam reports on on-going consumer boycotts, and provides a forum for manufacturers' responses. Grapes, jeans, gasoline, wine, fish, airlines—hardly any product or service category is immune from consumer protest action. So great is the collective consumer rage against Exxon, for its irresponsible handling of the Alaskan oil spill, that Exxon is not only a major target of consumer boycott, but also its very name has become synonymous with irresponsible destruction. "Exxoning" has entered the American vocabulary as shorthand for "messing up in a major way."

Environmental groups protest aerosols; groups like MADD (Mothers Against Drunk Driving) work for responsibility in the sale of alcoholic beverages to keep drunk drivers off the roads; grass roots groups spring up to preserve local resources; neighborhood groups even organize to promote neighborhood interests (NIMBY—Not in My Backyard—is the rallying cry). In Greenwich Village, local residents protested a proposed "prison barge" to be docked in the Hudson River, just steps from an elementary school. Boycotts have been fine-tuned for instant political clout. Protest was used with dartlike precision and lightning speed when pro-choice groups all over America threatened to stop buying Idaho potatoes if the state's governor signed a stiff anti-abortion bill. (He vetoed it.)

There are even protests to protest protests. When country torch-and-twang singer k. d. lang—a Grammy winner and animal-rights activist—appeared in a "Meat Stinks" ad campaign backed by People for the Ethical Treatment of Animals, she faced a boycott of her own: country music stations in cattle-raising states refused to play her records. One Sioux Falls, South Dakota, station gave away filet mignon every time it played a lang song.

Consumers are screaming. Smart marketers are listening. Success stories make heroes out of consumers and companies alike. And herein lies the crucial lesson in The Vigilante Consumer trend: it's not the *mistake* a company makes that the consumer finds unforgivable (at least for the most part), but how the company responds to the discovery of the mistake. (It's best, of course, if the company discovers it itself.)

Deep at the heart of the Vigilante Consumer trend is a wish that companies could somehow be more *human*. Consumers are willing, even eager, to say "anyone can make a mistake . . . after all, you're only human"—if that, in fact, is the way the company responds. It's not so much "what happened" but whether or not you fix it—quickly, responsibly, and honestly.

Take two case histories, albeit quite different in nature. Tylenol was faced with big trouble (through no fault of its own) when criminal tampering led to tragic deaths by poisoning. The company response was immediate, straightforward, and consumer-concerned to the point of self-sacrifice. Their company chairman spoke frankly, making no attempt to cover up the story; instead pulling the victimized product from the shelves. Helping the FBI. Spending top dollar to devise tamper-proof packaging.

Decency was not its only reward—but Tylenol also made major gains in consumer confidence and loyalty. And sales.

Contrast that with the scandal at Perrier. When reports leaked out that the bubbly mineral water was benzene-contaminated (though arguably with insignificant quantities), the press was firing off conflicting stories about the nature—and extent—of the problem. The company offered no immediate explanation. Instead, the small problem began to grow, to blow up on a larger and larger scale. Next came the news that Perrier's famous bubbles were not natural effervescense springing from the famous source, but merely factory-pumped-in carbonation. Strike three: Barbara Walters revealed on national television that the source of Great Bear bottled water (a Perrier subsidiary) is actually a swampy place somewhere in New Jersey. Three strikes, you're out. Where Tylenol emerged from tough times a hero—with honesty and real concern for the consumer, Perrier lost consumer confidence altogether, and lost much of its market because of it.

The history of the Vigilante Consumer is a history of big losers and winners. How do companies meet the challenge? Coca-Cola ignored the basic rule of customer relations by never really asking the consumer what she wanted. The result? The fiasco of New Coke. To Coke's credit, they came right back with Coke Classic—listening to the consumer, mending fences.

First Star-Kist, then Chicken of the Sea responded to the protests of children and others who boycotted canned tunafish to save the dolphins that were being accidentally trapped by drift nets. You can now buy cans of "Dolphin Safe" tunafish (consumers proved themselves willing to pay a little more for the costlier process required to keep dolphins safe)—a happy result for kids, adults, dolphins, and tuna companies.

McDonald's responded to complaints about fluorocarbons in packaging from consumers—including a highly vocal "Styro-Wars" campaign organized by the environmental group Friends of the Earth. They'd agreed first to separate out and recycle (eventually phase out) the polystyrene "clam shells" and cups used to keep Big Macs warm and sodas cold. Kodak has also established a policy for recycling their disposable "Fling" cameras.

Reebok even pulled a TV commercial that pictured daredevil "bungee cord" jumpers leaping off a bridge when viewers called in to protest the scary scene. A Reebok spokesman said the spot was yanked "for the purpose of being responsive to consumers." And R. J. Reynolds abandoned its plans for a brand named Uptown when activists revealed that the cigarette was being targeted to blacks. Consumers learned, companies listened.

No one likes being fooled: The straight-arrow Volvo company slid in consumer confidence when one of their televison spots showed a reinforced Volvo winning a competition in which other makes of cars collapsed when run over by a monster truck. And this in front of a huge crowd. Unforgivable to The Vigilante Consumer.

And no one likes being ignored: the most horrifying extreme was Audi, which failed to listen to the many consumer complaints about sudden, involuntary acceleration and failed to make a full public disclosure about the alleged life-threatening malfunction. Until the problem became all too public. Real consumer suffering (for whatever reason) cost Audi its reputation and its sales.

The lesson: to remember that the corporation/consumer relationship is a relationship between human beings. Give consumers credit for knowing what's going on. Listen to what consumers want and say. Tell them what they need to know when they need to know it. Respond to the consumer's concerns and desires. Even in the face of market pressures, a company will find out that decency is not only the only way to behave, but decency can also be profitable.

There's something I call the Comedy Connection which points up small but subtle examples of sensitivity to consumer perceptions. Remember all those jokes you've heard on television about mattress tags, warning that it is a *serious* crime to remove the tag, and that it's punishable by law? Have you read a mattress tag lately? They now say something like: "It is unlawful to remove this tag, except by the *consumer.*" Not a reform that will change the world, but an example I enjoy.

One wonders how much the jokes about airline food had to do with the improvements we're seeing lately: United has a low-calorie (400-calorie) meal; Pan Am has "WorldClass Cuisine," ranging from lighter food to more exotic fare, like Cajun tuna and peppercorn lamb. Swissair's specialty meals include dinners for people with medical problems, such as liver or kidney trouble. I especially like the chocolate chip cookies some airlines are sky-baking for passengers—great taste, great aromas, great comfort—Cocooning!

Here is the future, Vigilante-Consumer-wise: the corporate aura of power and omniscience has been demystified. For years, consumers couldn't see the man at the top of the corporate ladder. Now we want him out front, and held accountable.

Markets are becoming niches, and niches are growing smaller. As this market miniaturization occurs, consumers gain more stature—and they know it. Corporations will have to act fast—to revolutionize packaging and distribution; to detoxify their products; to set standards for themselves that meet the standards of the consumer.

"New" will no longer be a compelling selling point—an amazing idea in the American marketplace. We've had new all our lives. Now new is old. "New improved" doesn't do much for consumers either, except to make them say out loud what they've always wondered: "Why didn't you make it good enough in the first place?"

What will make us buy one product over another in this decade is a feeling of partnership with the seller, and a feeling that we're buying for the future. Anonymous, impersonal selling—the old-style K mart—is over. Stew Leonard's, a lively food mart in Norwalk, Connecticut, is chockablock with signs of the owner's personality. Stew has instituted an atmosphere filled with personal notes and sayings, suggestion boxes, managers' names, employee profiles, samplings, contests, and fun all over his store. We want to buy from a *person* . . . a person whom we trust. Trust will be implicit in every purchase.

Interactive warranties for things like appliances, entertainment units, home-office equipment and high-end cameras will soon be faxed from the point of purchase to the manufacturer. Corporate reps will get in touch with consumers to find out if they're happy—within days of purchase. More consumer/corporate contact. And another way for the manufacturer to penetrate the increasingly impenetrable cocoon-fortress.

Guarantees will also have a new and expanded meaning, beyond a piece of paper that you toss in a drawer. When something goes wrong, not only will it be fixed faster, but the "loaner car" concept will be considered a basic consumer right—for telephones, home faxes, computers, and other essential items, as well as cars.

Return policies will no longer punish us for changing our minds. Mail-order packing will be easily reversible; an unhappy consumer can just turn over the pre-addressed mailing label and send it back at minimal charge. (One experience recently: mail-order shoes from Roaman's cost $13.45 to quick-ship. Didn't fit. A call to their 800 number for Returns yielded this information: "Wrap it yourself and take it to your post office." More trouble and expense—another $3.80 for parcel post—total, $17.25 to try on a pair of shoes.)

There will be no forgiveness of huge mega-corporations that hide behind huge and complicated corporate structures. Labels will become more important than ever before. We'll want to know (like Big Brother) a biography of the product and the ethics of the maker. We'll want to know the company's stand on the environment, how it regards animal testing, human rights, and other issues—rather than just a list of the ingredients or a glimpse of an image. Listed prominently on the label, 800 numbers connecting the consumer to the corporation will be a way of life.

Anita Roddick has built her successful Body Shop empire on a do-good principle that ranges from save-the-earth policies to no cruelty to animals to "trade, not aid" for native projects in remote lands. Hopefully, she'll be a prototype for other companies to follow. The first company in every product category to initiate these advances will pull ahead and force its competitors to follow suit. With The Vigilante Consumer doing the dictating, no corporation can afford not to listen. No corporation can afford to make wrong choices.

99 Lives

"It takes all the running you can do, to keep in the same place. If you want to get somewhere else, you must run at least twice as fast as that!" said the Queen.

ALICE IN WONDERLAND

It sounded like such a good idea. Freedom of choice! Infinite possibility! Permission to be anything we wanted to be! It was the ultimate expression of the American Way, but with a decidedly '80s difference. Somewhere along the line, we stopped thinking, "I can live *any* life I choose" and started saying, "I can live *every* life I choose." And saying it with a certain swagger: yes, we *can* have it all. Everyone is SuperMan (or WonderWoman).

We ran through the '80s as a nation in a frenzy—FiloFaxes and phones in our hands, running shoes on our feet, babies at (some of) our breasts. Buoyed up with a kind of crazy ambition: to be as many people as we could possibly be. Multiple personalities and damned proud of it. Challenging the notion of time itself. Not to mention the limits of *energy.*

Recognize yourself? Hardly any adult alive today doesn't know the sensation of 99 Lives.

Granted, we didn't bring it *all* on ourselves.

At the very same time we were so frantically pursuing *lifestyle* as high concept, the basic fabric of our lives was undergoing radical change. Family, for a start. Just being a human being who was related to other human beings sometimes meant taking on roles and responsibilities not common to other generations. Like the growing number of single parents, who have to double up as both mother and father. (Tellingly, the number of single-father households has grown 82% since 1980, faster than any other type.) And, although there's no official tally, the numbers of gay men and lesbians parenting, through adoption, foster care, and sperm banking, have increased substantially over the past few years. Or Boomerang families—where the adult kids return to the nest, living at home and forcing *everyone* to redefine the family roles.

In 1990, there were over 20 million 18-to-34-year-olds living with one or both parents. Who pays the mortgage? Who cooks the meals? How many times does a mother have to play "mommy" when her kids come home for another round or still another round. Or, what if there's a second or third marriage with multi-sets of kids? How many bedrooms are needed then?

And then there's the issue of multiple jobs. There are those of us who *volunteer* for the multiple lives required by multiple jobs: people who work double-time for career advancement or personal ambition, and those who undertake two (or more) career lives simultaneously out of sheer enthusiasm. And then there are those of us who are forced into double-duty by plain and simple economics. (In May of 1989, 7.2 million people held multiple jobs, up 1.5 million since 1985.) Life's arithmetic used to be simpler: one job per family, one marriage, one house, one community for a lifetime, one crop of kids. Today, these statistics get multiplied over and over (what's *your* frenzy factor?). We scramble to keep up. We scramble to keep track. No wonder the "chaos theory" is the hot language of today's math.

And we have other crusades. To stay young, get fit, live healthy. Achieve self-fulfillment and conquer self-doubt. Win friends and influence people. Get rich, get smart, get ahead of the crowd. Accumulate toys and trophies, the badges of having lived. Save the planet, save ourselves. Test out the theory that nothing is impossible. So many goals, so little time!

Factor in the sheer weight of information that rolls in like great enormous waves. It makes life incredibly (and somehow insidiously) more complicated: it takes more than one lifetime to wade through one lifetime's data. (R. S. Wurman in his book *Information Anxiety* says the amount of available information now *doubles* every five years.) Let's face it, we have never been busier—fulfilling all our roles, chasing all our dreams, processing all our data-bytes—living our 99 Lives. And we have never lived *faster*—just to get it all done.

Time. "Now there's a fine concept," intones the voice of the '90s. It's not just that we don't have *enough* time. It's as if time itself has become, well, *faster* than it used to be. Immediate is really immediate—there isn't a chance to stop and take a breath. Consider this: we experienced the events of the Persian Gulf War *live* on TV—beginning with what looked like a brilliant display of fireworks. There's no *cushion of time*. Our own Secretary of Defense admitted to receiving a lot of his "intelligence" right along with the rest of us from CNN. It changed our sense of time, it redoubled our load of stress.

The "speed of technology" brings us the facts of life faster than we can assimilate them. And information technology not only makes information instantly accessible to *us* at all times— it also makes *us* accessible to the information. We are, often quite literally, "on the line" much of the time. Nowhere to run to, nowhere to hide. We carry our telephones around with us. One quarter of American homes have cordless phones (more than 9 million sold in 1989 alone); 3.5 million of us have phones in our cars. (Hertz intends to have 45,000 in-car phones by 1995. Avis has them, too.) We even have phones to carry around with us in our briefcases. (To be honest, I couldn't live without my Mitsubishi 3000 now.) Adding to this instant accessibility are answering machines and call-forwarding/call-waiting features. There's just no excuse not to be reached. The only safe-from-incoming-calls cocoon we have left is the airplane in mid-air—and I expect even that will change any moment.

Consider the time transformation wrought by the fax for sending our *written words*—even our most intimate scribbles— around the world with the speed of electronic impulse. We are faxing at such a frantic pace—to send letters, to replace phone calls, to shop, to order food, to play pyramid games, to respond to magazine surveys, to request favorite songs on the radio, to carry on commerce—that the world's production of fax paper can't keep up. (Consumption of thermal-coated fax paper is growing faster than the available coating-plant capacity, and International Resource Development, Inc., warns of sharp price increases and spot shortages to come.) Increased convenience, yes, but we've lost that great playing-for-time excuse, "It's in the mail." We've lost those little "grace notes of time" we used to have while we waited for the news to get from here to there. The same advances we love for *giving* us time are so electron-speedy, electron-greedy, they're taking our time *away*. They're contributing to the Acceleration Syndrome that's driving us out of our still-in-human-time minds.

So what's the antidote to the stress of 99 Lives? It's Cocooning, or Fantasy Adventure, or Small Indulgences, or Cashing Out—or it's that customized-for-99-Lives salvation we call Streamlining. We don't want more *anything* anymore. What we want now is less. More and more less. Many of us never tape TV shows because: 1. It means we have to crack the secret Asian instruction manual code. 2. We have to learn to program the VCR. 3. We don't have time to watch the taped shows anyway. We're pleading to the big time clock in the sky: "Give me *fewer* choices, far fewer choices. Make my life easier. Help me make the most of my most valued commodity—the very minutes of my life."

The Week-at-a-Glance calendar leveraged time brilliantly in 1990, in a direct application of 99 Lives. Up until then, they'd slotted time each day for appointments from eight o'clock on. But starting that year, their appointment slots began at seven. Here's a company that gave its customers what they wanted—more time. Even if you never used the seven o'clock slot, or "scheduled" it for sleeping, there's an awareness factor at work: if you add up all the extra hours, their 1990 calendar year gave you two weeks more than the year before, two weeks longer than competitors' calendars that began at eight. Amazing.

We even see a certain streamlining in the arts. In the literary world, there's now "Flash Fiction"—short short stories by such writers as Amy Hempel, Diane Williams and Melinda Davis that are no more than two or three pages long. Sometimes a single page.

Americans have instinctively streamlined one time-intensive necessity of their lives: food. We have become a nation of grazers, eating several small "quick bite" meals throughout the day to replace the traditional sit-down three.

People are skipping meals and eating pretzels on the run. (Sales of salty snacks increased 5.1% in 1987 alone, to more than $8 billion.) Even those meals we gather round for, sit down for, are speed-prepared in some way or another: by 1987, the microwave oven had already topped the dishwasher as the most commonly owned kitchen appliance (who still uses dishes anyway, when they're grazing?). We spent $900 million on microwavable foods in 1989—by 1991, that figure should reach $3 billion. Speediest of all is someone else's cooking: home-delivered, take-out, or fast food (though in this age of speed-eating elevated to high art, even the term "fast food" seems hopelessly out of date). According to a Gallup Poll, about half of the 86% of Americans who eat dinners at home during the week are eating pre-packaged or take-out food that they pick up or have delivered. (Experts predict take-out food spending will rise at three times the rate of total food spending.) In Stamford, Connecticut, you can buy professionally catered, microwave-ready pre-packaged meals from a truck at the railway station. The name of the business: "Hi Honey, I'm Home." Fax Grande Cuisine in Elmsford, New York, accepts faxed-in menu orders that can be picked up by returning-home commuters at their suburban train station. Even the giant General Mills is experimenting with bring-it-home prepared meals: Bringers, a line of bistro-type fare, is being tested in select areas of Minneapolis.

Fast food for the '90s will be even faster. How about the Pizza Anytime machine, which dispenses pizza at the touch of a few buttons? Insert cash, select toppings, and the speed-pizza machine delivers your conveyor-oven pizza within three and a half minutes. There's one at Disneyland. Or the Touch 2000. Punch in a food order on a touch-sensitive countertop menu, and an IBM PC relays the order to the restaurant kitchen and cashier. Carl's Jr. restaurant in Azusa, California, has it. Even in Paris, you can buy a fresh-baked baguette from street-side vending machines at 350 locations!

What we're waiting for, hoping for, is a speedup of home appliances. Restaurants can steam-clean a load of dishes, glasses, and flatware in eight minutes. Why does it take our dishwashers an hour's worth of energy (and noise) to complete the task? Ditto for clothes washers and dryers.

The watchword for the streamlined '90s will be *multi-function*. Products that accomplish two or three things at once, or that allow you to get more than one job done at a time. The biggest idea is *cluster marketing*. Why should we have to make one drop at the dry cleaner, another at the tailor, a third at the shoe repair, and so on? Cluster marketing could bring it together: all-in-one service stops, like a parking lot valet service (with pickup and delivery), or a kiosk sited on the ground floor of office buildings.

Why not, in fact, provide more services in offices themselves? Gourmet meals to go wheeled in on coffee carts at around five o'clock—perfect take-home dinners for you and your family. Or, flowers on Friday? There could be cocoonlike "home rooms" (remember, office gyms seemed unlikely once, too), where manicurists, hairdressers, tailors, and retailers could come at lunchtime, to streamline our lives.

Espresso Dental, in Seattle, is a triumph of multi-function: the world's first combination dentist's office, espresso bar, and massage parlor. Suddenly, leisure time and dental hygiene are collapsed into one time slot! In New York City, VideoTown Laundrette has a tanning room, an exercise bike, copying and fax machines, and 6,000 video titles to rent, in addition to its laundry facilities. (It also serves popcorn for grazers.) BrainWash, in San Francisco, is a laundry/café that caters to a neighborhood crowd of artists and poets. McDonald's is testing a McExtras concept, where you can buy basics (milk, eggs, bread, etc.) along with Big Macs at the counter or drive-up window. This multi-function idea can provide a big opportunity for packaged goods marketers: how to combine benefits of two (or three) of your products into one.

Speed service is another growth area. Automated tellers are already dispensing stamps, transit tickets, and even shopping mall gift certificates (in addition to cash) in locations across the country. Press Box News, a Lancaster, Pennsylvania, company, is franchising its drive-through morning newsstand service: you can pick up your daily papers, coffee, and cigarettes without ever leaving your car. Why not more of these no-stop shopping outlets? The

Sixth Street Marketplace in Richmond, Virginia, makes it possible to shop by fax: you fax in your shopping list, their employees do the shopping, charge purchases to your credit card account, and deliver the goods the next day. (Why not the same day?)

Beyond speed service, how about just more service in general? Give us the ability to delegate away one or two of our 99 Lives. Not only more and better child care, but more and better elderly care? Parent care? More pet care services: beyond walking and vacation-kenneling, how about grooming, nutrition and behavior counseling, and minor veterinary tasks, all from the same all-in-one, personalized service? There are local entrepreneurial services that offer a helping hand to do what used to be "wifely" chores: gift purchasing, party planning, multi-stop grocery shopping, larder stocking, spring cleaning, wardrobe shopping—even paint-color choosing and waiting for repairmen. Why not a national franchise, like Roto-Rooter?

And how about information editors? I see the beginnings of it here and there already: MovieFone, an interactive phone service with a taped directory of theaters, films, and show times, to reduce movie-expedition-planning to a single call. Or Manhattan Intelligence, a subscribers-only resource for information on everything you can do, see, eat, buy, whatever, in the city. The biggest technological achievement of the 99 Lives era will be a way to *edit down* all the information that assaults us daily. Maybe a computer that scans selected publications and edits out information we want or need to know, based on intimate knowledge of our lives, our tastes, our inclinations. That scans and edits our mail!

The lesson to everyone from 99 Lives? Edit. Cut back. Pare down. Simplify. Streamline. Not so much so that we can all live even faster (packing more and more into one day), but in order to be able to live *slower* again. Achievement without exhaustion. Accomplishment with less stress. I'm sensing a whole new TimeLine for the '90s. We still want to get ahead, but what if it takes ten years instead of five? Do we really want to switch spouses? Would corporation B really be all that much better to work for than corporation A? Are all 99 Lives really worth all that stress?

What we really want is to buy back time. Marketers that help us do that will be all-time winners.

S.O.S.
(Save Our Society)

S.O.S. is our front line of defense against the apocalypse.   1986

Maybe it's the last line.   1989

We can never give up the belief that the good guys always win. And that we are the good guys.   1991

To understand a society, learn about the society the way a child does: the early conditioning, the schooling, the rules of behavior, the basic lessons of childhood. To understand a society's *future*, listen to the questions the children then ask.

Look at the preoccupations of children today. It is a generation I have been calling Survivor Kids—because surviving is their primary business. At the most deprived and tragic end of the social spectrum are "underclass" kids who are truly forced to struggle just to *survive* in the world: abandoned AIDS and drug-addicted babies, cast-off and neglected children, the children of economic and social catastrophe, the babies of babies themselves. Kids who *are* cared for have survival of another kind on their minds: what is going to happen to the planet? To civilization? To the human race?

The rosy-future doctrine and the almost-religious belief in "Progress" that we teach American children is just not jiving with what they see around them. They are watching the destruction of the earth on the evening news. Beyond the news, they have their own environmental TV shows, like "Network Earth" and "Captain Planet and the Planeteers"; their own save-the-earth magazines, like *P-3* and *TLC*; their own books, like *50 Simple Things Kids Can Do to Save the Earth*; their own clubs, causes, grass roots organizations. A kid prevented from playing outside because it's a bad air-quality day takes air quality seriously.

The question of the survival of the world is *the* issue for this soon-to-take-over generation. It unites them. It politicizes them. It scares them to death. And it's the driving force behind S.O.S., the "Save Our Society" trend.

I begin with children, because here is where I see the greatest hope. And this trend has to have a hopeful premise. For all of our sakes.

What is the S.O.S. trend exactly? It's any effort that contributes to making the '90s our first truly socially responsible decade: the Decency Decade, dedicated to the three critical E's, Environment, Education, and Ethics.

It's consumers acting one by one to clean up their own acts—but more than that, it's recognition that individual action isn't enough any more. We want someone to take charge. (Who is running this planet, anyway?) A big part of the unease we feel about our predicament—about the Deadlines we see moving inexorably toward us—is a sense that there is no one out there to save us. And we're right.

The truth is, it's too big for one savior to handle. There has to be a collective action. And that action, though spurred and buoyed up by individuals, must be led by the big power structures that be. In America, like it or not, that means our only hope is in capitalists-for-decency; moral transformation through marketing.

Survivor Kids, when they take over, will demand it and make

it happen. But we can't wait to turn the world over to them. We may have committed societal and global suicide by then. What can we do? What are we doing now?

Here are some strong positives. Awareness of the need to save our society is at an all-time high. There is no such thing as a "we didn't know" excuse anymore. We've all seen enough *Time* and *Newsweek* cover stories—enough TV specials and speeches—to know our planet and its people are in dire shape. (Imagine the staff meetings at newspapers or magazines. "What! Global warming! The greenhouse effect! Political ethics! We can't run *that* again!") Our most urgent news is old news now. The danger is that emergency warnings turn into clichés. Cynicism sets in. Or a feeling of powerlessness. (*How* many barrels of oil are floating out there? I can't *think* about it.)

Doing good is no longer an option—it's a must.

Another phenomenon in our favor is the aging of America.

The predominant vision in the country now is coming from middle age—a time when nearsightedness turns to farsightedness. Even as we're Down-Aging, we're thinking ahead, turning from short-termism to long-termism. We've taken from the world, and now we want to give back. In other words, the prevailing cultural biological clock is beginning to say it's time to be good. And saying it just in time.

More good news: the battle is underway. Maybe not a true ground swell of mass effort, but enough collective action to inspire optimism. We have turned our forward motion in the right direction. The future is in pushing these beginning efforts further and further.

The best news for the environment is the growing recognition that decency can be profitable—and increasingly (we hope) tax-deductible. Think of the companies that stand out—both morally and financially—in the past few years: Ben & Jerry's, The Body Shop, Patagonia, Tom's of Maine. They all started with social responsibility above profitability as the primary goal. Consumer demand is the pull. Company commitment is the push.

Within a week of the introduction of its "green" line, Canada's Loblaw supermarket chain sold an astounding $5 million worth of phosphate-free laundry detergents, biodegradable diapers, bathroom tissue made from recycled paper, and coffee filters that don't release chlorine. Procter & Gamble is packaging several of its products—Tide, Cheer, Era, Downy, and Dash—in 25% recycled plastic containers. You can now buy paper carton refills of Downy. Colgate-Palmolive has soft plastic pouches of Palmolive Dishwashing Liquid to refill a reusable jug.

Wal-Mart stores have a company-wide green policy: publicly calling for more environmentally friendly products from vendors, highlighting green products with tags on shelves, setting up recycling centers in the parking lots of their 1,522 stores. General Motors has announced commercial production of the Impact, an electric car that produces no emissions at all and can run for 125 miles before its batteries need recharging.

The obvious S.O.S. directive here: if you're a company, *take* these kinds of actions; if you're a consumer, *support* these kinds of actions. It's the future.

Nearly one half of Americans have taken some kind of environmental consumer action in 1990: 54% stopped using aerosol sprays, 49% bought products made from recycled materials, 34% reduced their use of paper towels, and 34% didn't buy a product because of concern for the environment. Various environmental "seals of approval"—the Green Seal, which bases its environmental acceptance on a product's entire life span; and the Green Cross, which verifies manufacturers' environmental claims—will soon help educate and guide consumers in making green purchases. (Other countries are ahead. Canada has an Environmental Choice seal; West Germany's Blue Angel is already twelve years old.) There's also a catalog listing ecological products called *Seventh Generation*. And *Shopping for a Better World*, a guide for "socially responsible supermarket shopping," that's already sold 700,000 copies to motivated consumers.

Environmental basics are finally beginning to be perceived for just what they are: basic. Like recycling: more than 800 pieces of recycling legislation were introduced in 1989 alone. There's even a new consumer magazine dedicated to the waste problem called *Garbage*. Curbside recycling is now the law in many communities. Voluntary recycling is growing and growing. It takes a month for paper to decompose in a landfill, 500 years for glass and aluminum to decompose. It takes three minutes a day to separate the average household's paper, glass, and aluminum for recycling.

And the Good Guy is back! Our whole idea of heroics is changing. We're going beyond knighting the richest, the cutest, the most powerful, the sexiest. We are also saluting the Ethical Man who makes it his business—both literally and figuratively—to make the world a better place. Timely heroes!

Consider these candidates:

There's John Adams, co-founder and executive director of the National Resources Defense Council, the private organization (called the shadow EPA) that brings together scientists and lawyers to investigate—and litigate—environmental crime: air, pesticides, drinking water, public lands, forestry, coastal-zone management, global warming, and all other issues that get their attention. The NRDC has become a major public-policy player, helping pass such important laws as the Clean Air Act, the Clean Water Act, and the Toxic Substances Control Act—even organizing teams of American and Soviet scientists to monitor nuclear testing.

Paul J. Elston of Long Lake Energy Corporation—known for playing David to energy's Goliaths—challenges big utilities by building and operating independent alternative-energy plants, providing more energy for less money and with less waste than conventional utility plants. Andrew Cuomo, son of New York governor Mario Cuomo, left his job with a Manhattan law firm to donate his time, full-time, to HELP, an organization he founded to bring government and private developers together to build non-profit housing for the homeless. Psychiatrist Mitch Rosenthal is the driving force behind New York City's Phoenix House, the pioneering, therapeutic community for drug abusers.

Carole Isenberg and Lynda Guber, two former New York City schoolteachers turned Hollywood writers and producers (as well as wives of big studio chairmen), cofounded Education 1st!, an organization dedicated to improving education through entertainment resources. Their project grew out of motherly concern: the public school in the neighborhood was so undermotivated, they didn't want to send their children there. Today, their committee includes such L.A. heavy hitters as Brandon Tartikoff, Eric Eisner, Jon Peters, Laura Ziskin, and Joel Schumacher. Among other things, they try to influence television executives to include proeducation story lines and images in network programming.

And Anita Roddick, of The Body Shop International, goes to inspiring limits to make cosmetics (and cosmetic packaging) that are as caring for the environment as they are to the consumer. (Since traditional paper-making techniques are destroying forests, she has set up workshops in villages in Nepal to start an industry producing shopping bags and gift tags from a "paper" made of banana leaves and water hyacinths.)

And there are the bigger Good Guys, too.

Rubbermaid has just initiated an environmental program dedicated to "Helping the Earth Bounce Back." Ernest & Julio Gallo has donated money to the American Forestry Association's Global ReLeaf program: the aim is to plant 100 million trees in the United States by 1992 to counteract the greenhouse effect.

Cornell University's School of Hotel Administration is offering a course on "Housing and Feeding the Homeless." Habitat for Humanity, whose volunteers include Jimmy Carter, has built 5,000 homes for America's poor since 1973. The Community Capital Bank in Brooklyn is one of the nation's few full-service banks focusing on social responsibility. It makes capital available for the construction of affordable housing and for small businesses. And New York's largest law firm, Skadden, Arps, Slate, Meagher & Flom, has established a $10 million fellowship program to represent the poor in lawsuits: helping the homeless, assisting families in divorce and child custody disputes.

Outward Bound in New York City has a program with corporate sponsors (AT&T and Chase Manhattan Bank, among others) to help make school a more exciting place for students at risk of dropping out. Coca-Cola has targeted education as its "philanthropic focus"; it has given over $50 million to educational charities. Actually now one third of U.S. corporations are providing courses in reading, writing, and arithmetic to new employees who need them.

Volunteerism is up. Nearly half the American population now volunteers for such things as raising money to fight disease and to assist the poor, elderly, or disabled. There's been a tremendous surge in "helping hands" for AIDS hot lines and hospices—and more recently, for veterans' hospitals.

About 600 American corporations have employee volunteer programs, up from only 300 ten years ago. Xerox has instituted a "Social Service Leave," which allows any employee who's been with the company three years or more to take on a 3–12-month project with a nonprofit organization while being paid full salary. And K mart has its store-organized "Good News Committees," which take on local charitable efforts.

Rather astonishingly, charitable giving rose 92.2% between 1980 and 1987. Though equally interestingly, in 1990, American households with incomes of less than $10,000 gave an average of 5.5% to charity; those making more than $100,000 gave only 2.9%.

What's in the future? I predict a new ethic of self-sacrifice on the part of Americans. If only one member of every family would dedicate himself (or herself), not to the priesthood as in former eras, but to serve in the fields of education, health, the environment, social concerns.

Already we're seeing enrollment swelling in social concerns: a 10% to 15% increase in graduate schools of social work in 1987; a 61% increase in enrollment in teaching programs from 1985 to 1989; a greater expression of interest in public service careers. Hopefully, the people holding the most prestigious positions in the future will once again be the doctors, scientists, educators, and social servers. Those who do the most to benefit other people.

And we should see more good coming down from "above": in a capitalist move toward decency. The S.O.S. maxim: let the concerns of the nation become the concerns of the corporation. IBM is already giving computers to classrooms; Apple, to ecological groups. But soup companies should run free soup kitchens. Clothing companies should donate clothes to the poor. Toothpaste companies should start dental clinics for needy children. The publishing industry should plant trees. Car companies ought to provide transportation to the old, the young, the disabled. We need to start taking care of each other again.

The American marketplace, as we know it, will be transformed. Consumers will demand—and search for—products that not only work the best, but those that offer some "just" benefits.

The ultimate concept: Cause Marketing—where each purchase expresses a point of view about the environment, social issues, even political candidates. Included in the cost of goods to the marketer is money that goes to support an admirable cause.

Where to start? If a product pollutes or destroys, stop buying it and tell the company that's what you did. Suggest that while they're solving the negatives, they should look to create some positives: products and services in the true spirit of S.O.S.

Look for ways to become a Good Guy. Really recycle. Help your kids do their homework. Contribute time and/or money to the homeless. Be ethical. Do good.

S.O.S. is a do-good, be-good trend. Still in the hope-and-possibility stages. Become the person that leads the movement in your family, in your company, in your neighborhood.

Do right.

It isn't enough just to "do no wrong."

THREE

GETTING ON-TREND

BrainReserve's Trend Techniques and How You Can Use Them to Bring Your Business into the Future

Imagine a language with *only* a future tense. That's TrendTalk.

BrainReserve 101:
Consulting in the '90s

Predictions based on trends are not ivory-tower ideas. Hocus-pocus prognostications. Nor are they foggy crystal-ball readings. At BrainReserve, there's a methodology to our so-called "madness." A methodology to analyze and to apply the trends. To come up with sound marketing answers for our corporate clients. For new products, new names. Second opinions. Revivals of dying brands. And, above all, for a profile of the future consumer.

Basically, we're in the business of ideas; of funneling problems toward solutions. We're set up to hypothesize and refine our ideas by holding them up to our three main sources of information: the ten trends (our TrendBank); the "reserve" of creative thinkers (our TalentBank); and consumer interviews (over 3000 nationwide per year). By using these diverse wells of intelligence, we can quickly see if our ideas need to be adjusted left, right, up, down. We can gauge if the ideas will work their way into the future. We can project if the ideas will end up in consumers' homes, in their lives.

As always, the trends are our ultimate fail-safe.

I'm always amazed at how many people imagine that we sit around at BrainReserve dreaming up "pie in the sky" products or "way-out" predictions. The solid core of our business is based on substantial, long-range projects that we've been specifically hired to do, such as what we call FutureFocus: (the Future of Food, the Future of Fast-Food, the Future of Film, and the Future of Brand-Name Drugs). Some assignments are incredibly tough, such as Brand Renewal: finding viable solutions to reviving a tried and true but no longer wanted brand. At times, it's our task (second opinion) to tell clients that their exciting new "technology-based" product is not consumer-friendly. Actual case: (How many people would want a bright wall paint that never faded—but could never ever be painted over?) And a small, but fun, part is business we generate ourselves by thinking of viable ideas and matching them up to the right clients. Or, by "discovering" products on the fringe and recommending that our clients "mainstream" them.

Some ideas come from the way we monitor the daily news. We generally read business-related articles in an interactive framework, as if we're having a conference with the corporate players. "What has happened to your business?" "What can we do to help?" Often the most clear-cut answers are derived when businesses are "on the rocks" or in some kind of trouble.

Disaster on one side usually spells opportunity on the other.

Early in 1990, we read about the Perrier recall. That was the bad news. What we saw was the good news: an opportunity for San Pellegrino—or any other mass-distributed mineral water.

This reasoning has a precedent. Nearly a decade ago, Michel Roux of Carillon Importers spotted such an opening during a consumer boycott of Russia and Russian products. Since the top-selling upscale vodka was then Stolichnaya, he saw a way to turn the negative "don't buy Russian" slogan into a positive for his company's relatively unknown import, Absolut. After a brilliant advertising blitz, no one questioned whether or not a vodka from Sweden was best.

Absolut captured the market. It's the premium vodka of choice.

In an entirely different area, I remember reading about Reebok's air-pump running shoes, which got me thinking about the one thing I hate about running shoes. Since I travel a lot (and run on the road), these enormous shoes take up almost a quarter of the suitcase. It led me to thinking—why not truly inflatable running shoes with a mini air pump for travelers?

As it happens, some of these ideas lead to assignments (others not). More importantly, ideas lead to other ideas and, eventually, to a new reality. As a reminder, I keep a simple but very direct sign on my desk: "It Can Be Done."

Our first documented record of BrainReserve ideas ran in the *New York Times* in 1980. It was entitled: "Inside Consumers' Minds." And we use it as a benchmark, not to brag that we were right, but to show that we understand the marketplace. It seems very simple: predictions are early-warning signs. If a company stops to listen to consumer trends, it can gain a competitive edge.

—We said that Americans, newly warned about cutting down on salt, would miss its taste and look for alternative ways to replace it. What happened? Fresh herbs in the supermarket. Spicy foods everywhere—from fast food to frozen dinners.

—In looking at the endless parade of bland, boxy, and stripped-bare American cars, we said that many people would "miss the glamour of the flashy car . . . so watch for the little car laden with razzmatazz, but good on mileage." Look what's here. The new Mustang, the Miata, the Celica.

—We also predicted a shift away from wine and a return to thirties' glamour cocktails. The Sidecar's not back yet. But the martini is.

—We said that the divorce rate would go down (it did), fidelity, up (yes, post-AIDS). And there would be renewed interest in the family (there is). We're now experiencing a new baby boom and a return to religion.

—We said that the focus would swing away from the "Youth Culture" to middle age and beyond. Remember how revolutionary "The Golden Girls" seemed when it was first aired? A show about the fun and foibles of four older dames. It's still in the top ten.

The *Times* called our findings "controversial."

Since then, we've quipped and been quoted as foreseeing: the return of the Barcalounger; the rise in home media rooms; Nouveau Italian as the most popular restaurant fare; the yogurt market as secure, Tofutti, shaky. And more—at-home offices; electronic agendas; anti-stress center bathrooms; leaner beef; water bars, coffee bars; sugarless toothpaste; and fuller-hipped women.

The most press came in 1984 when we called New Coke "the marketing fiasco of the decade," and further added, "The giant kneels."

That our findings seem so obvious now is why BrainReserve's methodology works. It's proof-positive that you can start to create the future today. And start to profit from it tomorrow.

The trends take off your blinders. They open up your eyes— and give you TrendVision.

And that's the only way to see the future coming.

BrainReserve 102:
Packaging the Future

Looking for signposts to the future can be fun, but in the business of ideas, as in any other business, you can't just process the paperwork. You have to remember to stop and think. And think ahead. Or else you lose track of your own future.

At BrainReserve, we project far into the future and then look backward to see what's an appropriate action for our client at a particular point in time. It's like looking at the future through the other side of the telescope. If you know what's going to happen in the far future, it's pretty easy to determine the right thing to do in the present or the near future.

The future of consulting has changed considerably from the way it was when we started BrainReserve in the early seventies. Those were leisurely economic times. Corporations could afford to wait six to nine to twelve months for solutions; then take *years* to decide whether or not to act.

No one has that kind of leisure anymore, what with today's

tightened-up consumer world. There's a new urgency to the marketplace. We can feel it among our clients. And we've had to respond as well.

I'm always telling my *product* clients that they need to turn their businesses into *service* businesses—but what should service businesses do? What could they offer? Looking at the future of my own service-oriented company, I began asking myself that question.

One answer came to mind: we need to become a product business as well.

In addition to our consulting services, the product we're packaging is the future—trying to bring news and views of the future to more and more people. And the future can be packaged and positioned in any number of ways. In the planning stages: a TrendFax newsletter and/or a magazine, a how-to consumer guide on what's coming and what to do about it. Carol Farmer, the retail guru, even suggested we open a TrendStore, where we sell the newest on-trend products for one month only; no stock.

One of our most successful products now is a seminar called TrendView. We take groups of anywhere from 20 to 1500 people through an overview of the future. By giving examples of fads vs. trends, today's heroes, what's hot and not, we dimensionalize the trends with facts and figures as well as slides.

I usually open by telling a story about my name (if I don't, the audience is too preoccupied about the origin of "Popcorn"). It's usually a tongue-in-cheek tale about "my Italian grandfather"— Poppa Corne—whose name got changed at Immigration.* Then, I can go on.

The most illuminating aspect of the talk is to catch what prompted the audience to laugh. These sparks of levity usually prove, in hindsight, that the trends work. They're directions that lead to the future. It's always the very remarks that seem so

*The real story: my first real boss and still friend, Gino Garlanda, always had trouble (and fun) pronouncing my family name. He would go through variations of Plotkin—"Potkin, Papkin, Popkon, Popcorn." So he nicknamed me Popcorn— and I liked it. (Yes, Popcorn is on my passport.)

shocking or so absurd that eventually become so commonplace.

I've been told, time after time, that there's an executive refrain in many corners of corporate America that goes something like, "Faith Popcorn said this would happen years ago." At an international conference in Florida in 1983, I announced to the audience that a new disease called AIDS would soon impact the social interaction in America, changing not only the singles' bar scene (i.e., casual sex), but also the overall marriage/child-bearing rate. They started to snicker and then laughed (out loud), telling me that it would have *nothing* to do with their business—a food company.

This kind of nervous reaction seems to be a small, but inherent, part of TrendTracking. Many new ideas are jolting, especially when they haven't been factored into a company's ten-year projections or marketing charts. Of course, there's always a sense of satisfaction (revenge?) when clients tell me later that they should have listened. But in my business, you can never say, "I told you so."

For instance, at the start of the eighties, we suggested to a perfume company that American women would respond to scent with intense sexual power, beyond passion. BrainReserve's recommended name: Obsession! One packaged goods client thought that our trend projection of a healthier food for dogs was a totally stupid idea, until a competitor, Purina, came out with O.N.E., a health-driven product. (A former partner of mine, Peter Flatow, used to warn our clients, "If you're thinking about a good new product idea, then somebody else is probably working on that same bright idea, too. Or is about to.")

But what always amazes me the most are the companies that don't think they need to heed consumer trends. That it's only today, and not tomorrow, that counts. Usually those companies are located in Detroit.

Recently, a luxury car maker there told me that he didn't need us because he doubted that the consumer would ever believe a $30,000 American car could convey "luxury" in the same way BMW, Mercedes, or Lexus does. I explained that the consumer in the '90s did want luxury, but at a lower price. And if he positioned the car properly, it could be a winner. He retorted with the fact that his car still didn't have the quality, had a shoddy reputation, but was being improved. And that he needed to speak to someone who understood *cars*, not *consumers*.

This kind of short-termism in corporate American thinking is maddening—and knowing it's the primary reason Detroit is in the toilet makes my American blood run cold. (Not too long ago, this particular make of automobile was the nation's symbol of "I made it.") Too many marketers assume that the future will hold back and wait until they're ready for it. It won't.

How do you hold the future in your hands? Literally, in your hands. BrainReserve has created a product which we call TrendPack, or the future in 3-D. We box up a bi-monthly package of items that illustrate our trends—the ethnic/world music of Gipsy Kings; Terra Chips, crispy, colorful, thin-fried root vegetables (yuca, yam, parsnip, lotus, beet); a make-your-own-perfume kit; herbal energizer pills, even an honest-to-goodness crack vial (empty), plucked from an East Village rooftop—for a roster of a hundred culture-watching clients.

And because our clients increasingly want future-based answers fast, we've "packaged" still another product: BrainJam (yes, BrainReserve's big on turning two words into one), in-house meetings for quick, one-problem solutions. Named after free-flowing jazz improvisations, these one/two-hour sessions take up issues, amplify them, and solve them—right then and there. No pain, pure gain. There's an outside moderator (to facilitate the flow), plus a group of ten to twelve, made up of BrainReserve staff, TalentBank experts, and the clients themselves. In a short period of time, our clients catch the rhythm of the BrainJam sessions. And get their answers.

We "brainjammed" an internal problem of our own: what exactly is BrainReserve? How should we define ourselves? Position ourselves? We started out by saying that we are a marketing company, yet more. "A ThinkTank?" Not quite. "A consulting company for the future?" Almost right. Then someone said, "We're a small, caring *clinic* for future thinking." After mulling over the pros and cons of each and every word, we agreed. We all liked the take-care-of, concerned "clinic" image. Problem solved.

A slightly longer variation of these hit-and-run meetings exists when a client wants to explore a theme over a full day or two. Nissan requested one of our TalentBank Interfaces, and in the smart Japanese roundabout way asked not "What is the future of the premium car industry?" but "Tell us about the future of style." We assembled some of the top style-makers from our TalentBank: lifestyle author Martha Stewart; magazine editor Amy Gross, *Mirabella*; store designer Joanne Newbold; cookbook writer Lee Bailey; interior designer Birch Coffey; fashion designer Diane Benson; and so on. Our panel speculated, expounded, illustrated, and shared their "insider" opinions. Nissan walked away with a clean, clear view of American style, from all angles. On-trend truths, to ride into the future. Now let's see what comes rolling down the road.

What's BrainReserve's business is possible for your business. Starting here, you'll find out exactly how *we* apply the trends and how *you* can do the same. The practical application basically goes like this:

From a trend prediction . . .

To a trend production . . .

To a trend product.

The Trends Lens:
Discontinuity
Trend Analysis

At the heart of every project we do at BrainReserve is a process we call the "Discontinuity Trend Analysis." This rather formal-sounding process is the methodology by which we measure a specific target—an industry, business, service, product or product ideas, marketing/advertising concepts—against the trends. (We have even used this method to analyze such diverse targets as movie treatments/screenplays, publishers' book lists, magazine prototypes, proposed "heroes" and premises for new television series, celebrity spokespeople, and political campaigns.)

What we are basically asking are questions like these. Is the idea/product/concept continuous or discontinuous with the trends? Is it on or off? Will its appeal keep up with the needs and wants of the consumer? Is there longevity potential? Does it tap into a "deep stream" in the culture—or will it trickle off and go the way of a mere fad? In short, does this widget have a future?

Our expertise, beyond analysis, is in creating entirely new

concepts or rethinking existing concepts—not only to *fit* the trends, but to give them real expression. The big successes are the ideas that are supported by *at least four trends.* One trend— say, Fantasy Adventure, for example—may be the main driving force behind an idea; but the idea must also fit three or more other trends in some way.

Here's how it works. You begin with the trends themselves. Taking each trend, one at a time, you analyze the idea (the business, the product) against it. First, you look for clues of continuity/ discontinuity. Is the idea in tune with the trend (naturally) or at odds with it (if so, is the clash fundamental)? Is the idea basically on-trend, but with some trend-fighting elements? If the target is on-trend, you look for ways to accentuate the positive. If the idea is off-trend, you look for ways to correct it: with drastic changes, if there's a fundamental clash; or with refinements, if only certain elements wander "off-trend." Analysis is the first step, correction is the second.

Let's take the supermarket industry, as an example. Here's an industry that runs pretty much the way it has for decades: shopping carts, a numbing array of things to choose from, long checkout lines, unwieldy bags. Most of us regard going to the supermarket as one of life's grim but unavoidable chores. But "grim" and "unavoidable" aren't the kind of adjectives that signal an industry with a future. Supermarkets are in trouble. Let me take you through the "top layer" of a Discontinuity Trend Analysis—to show you how the trends can help you put a finger on the problem and direct you to a solution.

Discontinuity Trend Analysis: The Supermarket Industry Trend by Trend

COCOONING

Is there anything about the supermarket industry that brings to mind the serenity of the cocoon? No. People would rather be at home. The daunting size and glaring lights, not to mention the clash of shopping chariots, make supermarkets about as far from the cocoon as you can get. Off-trend.

FANTASY ADVENTURE

Food is one of the all-time great fantasy adventures, but supermarkets kill the fantasy. The average American supermarket has no excitement beyond the occasional chip-and-dip sampling table or parking lot clown; there's no sensuality or magic. Supermarkets are mundane. Off-trend.

SMALL INDULGENCES

You may be able to *find* some here, but the supermarket itself is hardly a Small Indulgence. More like a Big Burden. You deserve a trip to the supermarket today? Hardly. Off-trend.

EGONOMICS

What's personal about a supermarket? By definition, it's a mass market. You join the nameless, exhausted hordes wading through an endless array of products. There's very little service: no babysitting, no one to help, no recognition of your individual needs.

Supermarkets are designed to move volume—products and people. Not to be customized. Off-trend.

CASHING OUT

Stress is the primary psychosocial emotion you associate with a trip to the supermarket. Stress is the very thing that makes people cash out. Off-trend.

DOWN-AGING

Well, maybe. Shopping in terrain that has changed little since one's childhood can be (though this is a stretch) a nostalgia trip. There's a familiar comfort to walking up and down the aisles the way you did with your mother when you were a kid. There's a pleasure in seeing a lot of shapes and colors arrayed before you. Minimally on-trend.

STAYING ALIVE

Will the supermarket kill you? It might. It's a mine field of temptation. In a world assaulted by salt, fat, chemical additives, and pesticide pollutants, the supermarket is ground-zero. There's not enough information to give you a real read on what's healthy and what's not. And supermarkets just don't *feel* like Staying Alive kinds of places. Off-trend.

THE VIGILANTE CONSUMER

Most supermarkets feel like the prototypical consumer enemy. There's no one "out front" who cares about the consumer:

you are expected to make your way through a manipulative maze alone. The whole environment seems to say "We just put it on the shelves, lady. Take it or leave it." Plus supermarkets make it nearly impossible to shop politically, to make a statement with your dollar. There's no information about what's being boycotted (and why shouldn't there be? Whose advocate should the supermarkets be?); how to reach manufacturers for information and complaints; how to "buy green." To put it bluntly: consumers feel supermarkets are in cahoots with the manufacturers, to fool us, to pull the wool over our eyes, to make a buck. They are not on the consumer's side. And that's off-trend.

99 LIVES

Nothing streamlined here—except in favor of the supermarket. (Will we ever really trust those electronic-eye code-reading checkouts?) Supermarket shopping is a hassle, right down to the exhausting ritual of wheeling your cart to your car, unloading it alone, then struggling back to return the cart (or just driving off). (Not to mention *urban* supermarkets, where, unless your store delivers, you buy only as much as you can carry.) Supermarkets could be so *on-trend*. But they are off-trend.

S.O.S. (SAVE OUR SOCIETY)

No. There's no do-goodism here. Even returning soda cans is a punishing experience. There's more to *throw* away than to put away when you get home. And we still know too little about the planetary implications of the purchases we make. Off-trend.

Industry observers can tell you that supermarkets are not doing well right now. As a trend observer, you can see that supermarkets are heading for calamity—catastrophe! With the exception of some minor nostalgia value, the supermarket industry is dreadfully off-trend on every count. And this is the industry that *represents*, in many ways, the core of "consumerism." It should be aggressively *on-trend*, not off. If this dire prediction sounds extremist to you, remember when department store defenders were saying there was no need for department stores to change for the future. Where else, they said, would consumers go? As department stores are tragically finding out, consumers *always* find someplace else to go when they reach "critical mass of discontent"—when what they are being offered is out of sync with their lives, is discontinuous with trends.

Trend Correction

What is my vision for supermarkets? This prototypical American marketplace must *transform* itself into the prototypical *future* marketplace, in order to survive. There is little (as we have just seen) about the American supermarket that is worth prolonging into the future. There is little about it that would respond to the initiating of small reforms. What is called for is an entirely new way of accessing product, a new way that's in keeping with the major societal trends. One recommendation for the future of supermarkets (albeit far-out) would be through Virtual Reality.

The Virtual Reality Supermarket

Some call it "cyberspace," others call it "artificial reality." What Virtual Reality is, is a technology that makes it possible to synthesize a world—a 3-dimensional, touchable, feelable, hearable, visible, interactive world—through computer-generated images and sensation.

To enter this world, a person puts on some sort of special clothing (at the moment, gloves and goggles)—that gets connected to a computer the experts are calling a "Home Reality Engine." Gloves receive and transmit data (Nintendo has already licensed a simple version of it for its home games); goggles (some call them "eyephones") situate you by sight and by sound in the synthesized space. Pointing a gloved finger transports you through the space—grasping an "artificial object" in artificial space sends very real sensations back to you via the glove. Sounds very Star Trek, but Virtual Reality technology exists right now. (NASA and the military have the most serious applications at the moment.) Jaron Lanier of VPL Research in Redwood City, California, said in 1989 that Virtual Reality could be in people's homes by the turn of the century. And that, of course, is less than ten years away. Imagine the possibilities for a Virtual Reality supermarket—a super high-tech shop-at-home-for-home-delivery system. Let's look at what happens, trend by trend:

Cocooning. Safe in your own cocoon at home, you decide, at your convenience, to do your supermarketing. You don goggles and gloves, then lie back on your eiderdown comforter. You don't have to leave home, even get dressed. In your coziest flannel nightshirt, you embark on your . . .

Fantasy Adventure. Imagine yourself going off to a glorious summer roadside stand to buy produce. (You can even squeeze the tomatoes—and actually feel whether they're ripe that day, through your glove.) Point your finger toward Marrakech or Jamaica to look at the markets your spices come from. Visit a French bakery to scan the baguettes and croissants. (Who's to say "smell" won't be part of Virtual Reality soon?) Smile at the face of the friendliest butcher in Iowa as he shows you his best cuts of meat, before shipment to your store. (If you're really curious, take a look at the fields where the cattle graze.) See your butter and milk at the dairy, your bottled water at its pure spring beginnings. Then you'll order them with a different eye, a different attitude. Supermarket magic.

Small Indulgences. What could be more indulgent than a daily, ten-minute trip out of this world?

Egonomics. The "Home Reality Engine" is a smart machine, with intimate knowledge of you. If you're on a low-fat diet, it guides you to healthy shopping. It knows the ingredients you need to put into *your* chili recipe, and guides you down the "aisles" so you don't forget cumin, say, or beer. (Imagine a quick rundown on how to prepare a recipe—including a "hands-on" lesson in filleting, or kneading bread dough—plus a look at the finished product, with serving suggestions.) It knows your political bent and special concerns, and can flash updated information to you about "green" packaging or boycotts or changes in kosher certification. With Virtual Reality, you literally choose your own world. You get to decide what you want to be real. Could there be a greater expression of customization than that?

Cashing Out. If you can't cash out to the country all together, you can at least "shop" at the Farmer's Market through Virtual Reality (and have your produce delivered directly to your home). In fact, just leaving the supermarket "rat race" to shop in comfort at home is a Cashing Out lifestyle triumph all of its own.

Down-Aging. The Virtual Reality Supermarket is real-life Nintendo shopping for adults, the ultimate toy. Fulfill your grown-up obligations while playing a really neat game.

Staying Alive. The Virtual Reality supermarket makes nutritional information instantly available to you—as well as information on food combining and menu planning (tailored to your family's needs). Learn healthful ways to prepare healthful foods, as you choose them.

The Vigilante Consumer. With complete product information always available to you, you are empowered to make informed choices. Interactive programs make it possible to speak back to manufacturers, and monitor the progress of promised reforms and company track records. "Labeling" possibilities are endless—there is no longer a physical limitation to size.

99 Lives. The total time you used to spend shopping is telescoped into the minutes you spend transported into Virtual Reality. Your purchases are delivered to you at home. You cover infinitely more "space" in dramatically less time.

S.O.S. (Save Our Society). While we may still "shop" for products dressed in fancy packaging and arrayed in lush displays on our screen, the manufacturers can now supply the goods stripped of superfluous packaging—and the actual purchases can be delivered to us almost "clean." We finally get the fun and hype of ideal shopping without the hassle and the assault on the environment.

The Virtual Reality Supermarket may still be future-future—which, in my time line, means fifteen years down the road instead of five. But it's where we're headed. Seeing this far ahead makes present-planning more intelligent—more future-directed.

Supermarkets should be thinking *now* of ways to segue into Virtual Reality tomorrow. This means putting capital spending into warehousing and delivery systems—not into new store designs; they'll soon be obsolete. It means becoming the *information-center* supermarket today, the supermarket known for personal service—to build a strong, believable foundation for the Virtual Reality supermarket it will have to become in the future.

Of course, Discontinuity Trend Analysis is not limited to solving the problems of existing industries. Here's an example of how we worked with Eddie Sardina, Freddie Piedra, and Paul Nelson at Bacardi Imports to develop a brand-new product, *Bacardi Breezers*—a low-alcohol, rum-based cooler with fruit juice—that is now (after less than a year on the market) the third-largest liquor brand in the country, selling over four million cases. Its phenomenal sales record is being touted in the press as a real "shocker." Liquor sales in general are declining, and wine coolers are experiencing a precipitous decline. To non-trend observers, Bacardi Breezers appeared to be a courageous launch. Those who were trend-wise, however, saw the smarts behind the concept.

Discontinuity Trend Analysis: Bacardi Breezers

Cocooning. The Socialized Cocoon requires newer and brighter ideas for casual home entertaining: a taste profile that is "away-from-home exciting," but effortless to prepare and serve at home. On-trend.

Fantasy Adventure. Rum carries with it its own resonances of tropical paradise and island adventure. The very name, Bacardi Breezers, sounds refreshing, light, and airy, like aqua-blue coves and wind-bent palms: the perfect updated fantasy for today's young and casual consumers. On-trend.

Small Indulgences. Quality at a fairly low price. The way a Bacardi Breezer is made makes it a perfect Small Indulgence. Refreshing and delicious, its good taste gives the consumer a sense of instant gratification. The first time you try it, you like it. On-trend.

Egonomics. This young and breezy lifestyle refresher was "made just for me." Minimally On-trend.

Cashing Out. It gives you permission to believe you've "left the rat race" for a dream place, if even for just minutes. On-trend.

Down-Aging. A drink that's dedicated to fun, fun, fun. On-trend.

Staying Alive. Fruity flavors, along with low-alcohol content, have a healthy halo. Minimally on-trend.

The Vigilante Consumer. A premium product from a trusted brand name with a track record for making consumers happy. On-trend.

99 Lives. You could make a good case that a "pre-mixed drink" is faster, easier than having to mix one. On-trend.

S.O.S. (Save Our Society). Low alcohol content makes it in line with current moderation trends. On-trend.

Usually, we look for a trend-fit across four categories—with one strong trend-expression fueling the concept. With Bacardi Breezers, you have a strong Fantasy Adventure statement backed up with nearly all nine remaining trends. We were not surprised at Bacardi Breezers' success. Applying Discontinuity Trend Analysis techniques to your ideas, projects, businesses, plans, can eliminate a lot of surprises for you, too. The first step is mastering a technique we call the Universal Screen Test.

The Universal
Screen Test

Analyzing ideas through a filter of the trends is more than a methodology for us: it's the way we look at the world. We have developed an almost instinctive means of trend-analysis we call "The Universal Screen Test"—and we don't read an ad, flip around TV channels, enter a new shop, or look at a poster without clicking into it. It's a sort of shorthand DTA—Discontinuity Trend Analysis. Not only does it help us measure the trend potential of whatever we happen to be looking at—it also helps us see trends emerging. And it's a way of culture-scanning—a sort of speed-reading technique—giving us the means of sorting through the great bounty of data we are all served up everyday.

Consider this: the average American is confronted with nearly a quarter of a million advertisements every year, plus countless hours of radio, television, conversation (our own and snippets we hear or overhear), jokes, songs, magazines, newspapers, books, billboards, menus, catalogs, direct mail solicitations, "You have won a million dollars" mailings, notes, letters, postcards from here and there. And this is just *language.* What about the visual parade of street fashion, shop windows, buildings, cars, animals, *mirrors?* (What can you learn from your *own* behavior?) No one can assimilate all that information. Most of us filter most of it out, according to some sort of unconscious screen or other—concentrating on things we think apply to our lives, ignoring things we think don't.

In the end, we tend to give our attention to the familiar—to things we already know. Most of us concentrate on the wrong things. By using the Universal Screen Test to sort input, you'll begin to recognize ways in which information that seems to have nothing to do with you might, in fact, have everything to do with you—and your business.

You'll be able to see your future.

Take the simple act of reading the newspaper. Let's say you own a small chain of stores in three states that sells CD's and tapes. You're known for your wide-ranging back-list, and your willingness to place special orders for customers in search of hard-to-find items.

You're reading the paper as we did one day, early in 1990, and you come across a full-page ad that nobody could miss. It's a Waldenbooks ad, introducing a new service called the Preferred Reader Program, with special savings for members, an 800# for ordering, and other services for customers willing to pay a nominal fee each year. You say to yourself how interesting this book-finding program is, then turn to the entertainment section to read the latest news in the music business.

Opportunity missed.

Instead, you filter the ad through the Universal Screen, and recognize what a terrifically on-trend idea this new Waldenbooks program is.

Cocooning: you order from home. *Fantasy Adventure:* an easier way to order books makes your favorite Fantasy Adventure reading that much more accessible. *Small Indulgences:* a small membership fee for special privileges is a Small Indulgence par excellence. *Egonomics:* you are a member of a special club; your personal tastes and needs are recognized and catered to. *99 Lives:* streamlined access to information, streamlined method of acquisition.

This program, you say, is dynamite. It enhances the core-business, but lifts it into the future by way of giving expression to five (count them) trends. Waldenbooks continues to be in the book business, but has smartly moved into the information-packaging business as well. That's the future.

If you're smart, you'll be ahead of your audio-store competitors, the first one to become a service/information business, with a Preferred Listener Program, special members' savings, a 24-hour 800# ordering system, and instant delivery. Maybe you'll have special Fantasy Adventure memberships. Or memberships that specialize in mood music, exercise instruction, stress-relief, and self-hypnosis for listeners who want help Staying Alive.

Or take another example. You own a drugstore in a Middle American town. You begin to notice, on laundromat billboards and in the back of the local college newspaper (a good sign—you're not just reading *Drug Store Age*) that there seem to be a lot of counter-culture mind-body happenings around in "normal" places. Yoga classes are being held at the nearby retirement home; a group in your neighborhood has organized to "chant" together once a week. You eavesdrop on a conversation in the local coffee shop about a woman who can cure your cold by massaging your feet. You see a flier that says for only $10, you can get a 20-minute anti-stress massage at your health club. About as far from your core business of toothpaste and Tylenol as you can get.

But no. Looking at this emerging local phenomenon, you see the intersection of several trends. What you might have ignored or scoffed at in the past, you now look at closely, through the test of the Universal Screen.

Staying Alive: for sure. All these seekers are looking for better health and longer life. *Egonomics:* counter-culture "medicine" is a major personality statement. It means you have chosen from all the choices in the world to find the individual answer that is right just for you. *Fantasy Adventure:* you're experimenting in exotic cultures, Oriental wisdoms. *Small Indulgences:* a $10 massage! *Down-Aging:* there's a certain return-to-the-sixties feel about all this. *99 Lives:* any effort to reduce stress speaks to this trend. And even *Cocooning:* any homey group that joins together to chant together is a pure example of the New Age Socialized Cocoon.

What is your response? You begin to think about ways to open your business to New Age medicine. Maybe it's as simple as a "special" on herbal teas in the cold remedies aisle. Maybe it's as ambitious as organizing small groups at your store in the evening to discuss holistic medicine and wellness: how to *avoid* using medication. A suicidal act? No! Not when "wellness" is the wave of the future. Not when you have opened up the opportunity of *two* markets, instead of just one.

Applying the Universal Screen can become as instinctive to you as to us. It's a shorthand method of organizing what you need to know about the world—and channeling that information into trend-true directions, for your business, for your company, for your life.

TrendBending

DEFINITION: TrendBending, n. The process of
shaping your product or strategy
around emerging trends.

Bending your product around a trend is like getting in front of a tail wind. Catch it right and its energy pushes you forward. Fast.

OR

Bending your product around a trend is like holding onto the mane of a horse as it goes from walk to trot to canter to full gallop. If you can hang in there, you're flying.

The secret to TrendBending is discovering what the trends have in common with the intrinsic qualities of your product and bending them around your product or strategy.

One example is our work (early 80's) on The Shower Massage

by Teledyne. These shower heads had sold well when they were first introduced, but gradually sales were slowing down. From our interviews, we discovered that people rarely gave much thought to the kind of shower head they had (unless when home-building or remodeling). Once in place, shower heads are simply taken for granted. In fact, consumer awareness of the product was so low that many didn't even remember that they already had a Shower Massage in their showers. And rarely used its adjustable features.

Three appropriate trends at that time were Concern for Wellness (which had evolved from Health/Fitness and would later become Staying Alive), Time Management (the late eighties would see it accelerate into 99 Lives), and Cocooning (in its second decade). Both Wellness and Time Management addressed the growing problem of stress. Within the Wellness trend, we were learning how stress kills, while in Time Management, we were realizing that "speeding up" was "stressing us out." Cocooning was a natural fit because consumers were seeking a safe haven to get away from it all.

Knowing this, we wrapped The Shower Massage around the *three* appropriate trends and positioned it as the ultimate at-home, anti-stress center. The body relaxer—tension reducer. A perfect TrendBend. The commercial that DDB Needham West created applied our findings by showing a beleaguered fully dressed executive so anxious to be pummeled into serenity that he jumped under his Shower Massage fully dressed. Sales soared that Christmas.

Based on the trends Staying Alive and 99 Lives, we recently bent a fast-food chain's strategy from Good Fast Food to Good Food Fast. Consumers will want to both eat well and conveniently in the '90s. The "well" part is the new news.

Another example: Stanley Tools wanted to market a tool kit to light-users. But what should they call it? What should be in it? Was it only for women?

The trends we bent around their proposed strategy were 99 Lives, Egonomics, and Cocooning. The briefcase-sized kit we developed was so basic, so handy, so easy to use (99 Lives); yet customized and complete with quality products (Egonomics); that for apartment dwellers (Cocooning) or any beginning do-it-your-selfers (women or men) it became an essential.

So, that's what we called it. *Essentials,* by Stanley. And that's what they made.

Bend your product around the trends and laugh your way straight to the bank.

The Extremism
Exercise

At BrainReserve, we never work toward a solution—we always go past it. We push the problem all the way to the end, to the blackest future possibility. The extreme. Then we let the trends help us work our way back to the solution. It's an approach we call Extremism, and it works for any problem.

If you were to apply Extremism to a hamburger fast-food chain, you'd begin by noticing that people are eating less red meat. What do you do? If you're working forward, toward an immediate patch-plaster solution, then you do what most fast-food chains have done—you'd diversify by promoting sandwiches of grilled chicken or fried fish, or you'd add a salad bar.

A year or two or five down the road, however, you might find yourself with additional problems: people are now worried about the salmonella in chicken, the health hazards of fish. And they're scared about hygiene and possible pesticides in the salads. You'd realize that red meat was only one symptom of a larger problem: that people are concerned, across the board, with what they're eating—consequently, with what you're serving. You're back to square one.

What you should do first is to face the problem (that people are eating less red meat) and project a time that people will be eating *no* red meat at all, nor poultry, nor fish. Imagine that everyone has become a vegetarian. Unlikely? Perhaps. Irrelevant from the point of view of a hamburger fast-food chain? No.

Then ask yourself, "What should we be doing now?"

Answer: You'll have to work your way back to the present, to the solution.

In the extreme, you could become the first fast-food chain with only all-vegetable products, like grilled vegetable platters and vegetable pizzas. You'd serve no meat (a business idea that will inevitably make someone rich in this decade).

Working your way back from the farthest point, you'd hedge your bets by offering vegetarian choices in addition to hamburgers. Good, imaginative ethnic vegetarian dishes, like cheesy nacho-burgers, veggie burgers on whole wheat rolls or Oriental stir-fried vegetable burgers (Sheratons, Disneyland, and the Hard Rock Cafes are already offering garden-burgers: onions, oats, brown rice, low-fat cheese, egg whites, and walnuts, at half the calories and one-fifth the fat of ordinary burgers). Being ready to go "green" will give you the flexibility to come out with a vegetarian line just when the public begins clamoring for it.

It would be a smart move. A right move. In working back to the present from the worst-case scenario, here's how the trends would map the way. A fast-food chain should reflect what the trends tell us people will want—Staying Alive (healthier food); Small Indulgences (good, inexpensive treats); Fantasy Adventure (out-of-the-ordinary tastes, variety); 99 Lives (time-saving, quick). If we want to TrendBend toward Egonomics (customization, quality), we might try adding a special premium filet mignon burger (smaller, richer). If used correctly, the trends can inspire a whole spectrum of options, of opportunities.

. . .

Try the Extremism Exercise on a small-business level, if you're a starting-out or struggling professional. Let the trends help crystallize your course of action.

—You're an attorney. But, in your community, there is an excess of able lawyers. All charging expensive hourly rates. Take that to the extreme: What would you do if no one hired you, no one could afford you?

You could become a kind of legal midwife, charging less for the standard variety of problems (Cashing Out/Egonomics). Extend the idea: initiate a phone-consultation service, charging your clients even less for giving uncomplicated advice by phone (99 Lives). You'll become the lawyer of choice; the attorney that most people need.

—Or, you're a doctor. Similar scenario. Costs are high, service is low. Between malpractice insurance for you and medical insurance for your patients, the profession seems to be emphasizing money over care. Hospitals are going bankrupt. Take it to the extreme: the whole system breaks down; people can't get help in a medical crisis.

What do you do? You might open a chain of Dr. Goodheart clinics with other like-minded doctors. Up-to-date equipment, but no-frills space. A small staff, with more medical assistants than M.D.'s. Budgets are kept under control. You'll try to duplicate what a country doctor did: let people walk in without an appointment or call you up (or 1990s-style—computer you or fax you) for advice and compassion. In some cases, you'll prescribe herbs instead of drugs. Make home visits. And for more serious cases, tell patients where to go for top treatment. (The trends in play: Cashing Out, 99 Lives, S.O.S., Egonomics.)

The Extremism Exercise works whether you're small potatoes or one of the giants.

—For a bigger case: suppose you're an American car maker and the numbers are down. The extreme: nobody will buy your model anymore.

Again, let the trends guide you back. One option is to create a Fantasy Adventure car that's a Small Indulgence, for people who have Cashed Out and don't need to travel too far. A friend of mine in the Japanese car business and I once invented a car which we whimsically called the PopSui, to be sold/serviced at supermarkets. The body of the car would snap together and have interchangeable seats—with unlimited color selection, even Dalmatian spots or zebra stripes (Small Indulgences, Down-Aging). The basic mix-and-match parts would always be in stock. The PopSui (Fantasy Adventure) would be wonderful on gas (S.O.S.), would be simple to repair (99 Lives), and would cost exactly $3,000 or 2 for $5,000. (Ford's experimental future car, the Ghia Zag, comes closest in looks to the PopSui.)

—Last example of Extremism: You're the IRS. You're already at the extreme: everyone hates you. People do anthing to avoid dealing with you. If there are small ways to cheat or hide a little taxable income, people will. There are few moral scruples against withholding information (or money) from you.

What do you do? You humanize the organization. You assign special representatives (tax doctors), available to the taxpayers, along the lines of personal bankers, the way they do in England. You upgrade your service; your 800 number is open 24 hours a day (99 Lives), and when taxpayers call you for help in preparing their returns, you actually help them. You make a person at the top the IRS spokesperson; he or she will go on TV every January, February, and March to give updated tax information to the public (Egonomics). You simplify the forms—this time for real. And best of all, you initiate a checklist and let the taxpayers choose where they'd like their tax money to go—for education, the homeless, ecology, drug abuse (S.O.S.) . . . or yes, even Star Wars.

We can't say it enough: go all the way to the extreme and let the trends bring you back. This methodology works. You'll come up with a product or service or new positioning that will be exactly right for this time and place. It's like what Wayne Gretzky, the famous hockey player, said when asked why he was so good: "I follow the puck to where it's going, not where it is or where it's been."

What we see coming now is not a great leap of imagination into the future.

It's simply *what's coming.*

Twisting the Familiar

One warm summer's day, when we were watching the world go by, it seemed as if every man, woman, and child had an ice cream cone clutched in their hands. "How clever a cone is," we thought. "How utterly convenient." Yet these carriers haven't really changed since they were invented at the World's Fair in St. Louis in 1904.

Why not expand on this handy, hand-held concept? Make taco cones and fill them with chili? or crisp rice cones piled with Chinese chow mein? Or English muffin cones cradling peanut butter and jelly, cheese and onions, or even an herb omelet?

This is Twisting the Familiar. Something comfortable turned into something new. Novelty without threat. It's a way of building on what the consumer already knows and likes, without taking away any of the benefits normally found in a favorite product.

Think of McDonald's Chicken McNuggets (much-loved fried chicken, only bite-sized, easier to eat). Or, Nabisco's Teddy Grahams (a double-twist: teddy bear charm enhanced by graham cracker taste and vice versa). Great ways to ease a wary consumer into new products.

Another way of Twisting the Familiar is with an exaggeration of the norm. The Alice-in-Wonderland syndrome.

- Giant sizes, such as huge mushroom-shaped muffins or plate-sized cookies.
- Miniatures, such as bite-sized pizzas, mini-Mars ice cream bars, baby veggies, espresso-for-one machines, itty-bitty Cuisinarts.
- New and different colors, such as tomato pasta, ink-black pasta, white bell peppers, hunter green KitchenAid mixers, sapphire blue gin.
- New packaging, such as the highly successful juice paks, or European mayo in a toothpaste-like tube (why not tubes of salad dressing base or salsa?).

The central premise of Twisting the Familiar is that the consumer world doesn't have to be the way it is. There are no absolutes. The trick is to challenge the assumptions, change the ground rules.

If you know that as many people like "salty" as "sweet," then look at some of the traditional sweets and ask why. Why are all frozen ice pops sweet? Instead of fudge or banana coconut, why not frozen V8 on a stick? Why are most yogurts sweetly fruit-based with globs of jam? Why not cool cucumber/mint or crunchy vegetable yogurts for lunch or a snack? And those diet shakes that are substitutes for meals. Why should you have to drink a sweet chocolate, vanilla, or strawberry dinner? Why not tomato-basil, herbal chicken, or wild mushroom, all closer to soup?

This works conversely, too. Why are most chewing gums spicy (cinnamon) or refreshing (spearmint) or child-oriented (bubble gum)? Isn't there an opening for a premium chocolate chewing gum (Godiva sugarless?), orange espresso or cappuccino gum?

Examine popular eating habits and you might find familiar twists. Plenty of people eat muffins for breakfast and slather them with butter and jam. Why not make life easier—and make microwavable muffins with a center nugget of butter and/or fruit preserves or chocolate spread. Or make cereal bars with a milky/creamy center.

If more people like hors d'oeuvres better than main courses, try creating a frozen dinner of mixed appetizers. And think of adding chunks of sun-dried tomatoes for texture or jalapeños for pizzazz to that familiar bottle of ketchup. (By the way, putting ketchup, mustard and relish in plastic squeeze bottles a few years back was perfect Twisting the Familiar.)

In other words, question everything.

- Why does shampoo come in bottles? Why not in bars, like soap?
- Why does cereal always come with two wrappings, inner bag, outer box? Why not just the bag, like Pepperidge Farm cookies? Or canisters, like bread crumbs? Or in big burlap bags, to be scooped out like oats or rice in days of yore? And how come no one has realized that cereal grains are sprayed with pesticides? Great opportunity for an organically grown cereal.
- Do Products really need to have packaging at all? Why do CD's need long double-size cardboard holders with plastic wrap when they come in their own plastic cases? The same with most beauty products?
- Why can't those brown padded mailing envelopes come with reusable closures?
- Why haven't cameras shrunk like calculators, so you can carry one around in your wallet? Or, why can't a camera double as a Walkman? Why aren't there cameras with mini-tape recorders in them so you can identify each shot (great for real estate agents, insurance adjusters, etc.)?
- Twisting the Familiar is letting your imagination wander across the marketplace. It's being free of fixed images, those static ideas of "It's always been this way." It's taking a hard look at everything to see what should be reshaped for this coming decade.

And it's reshaping things for a better world.

CAPITALIZING ON THE TRENDS

OBSERVATIONS AND APPLICATIONS

You can trust a crystal ball about as far as you can throw it.

Future KnowHow

No one knows (exactly) how the future will feel and unfold, but the trends are pushing us there with a force that's almost tangible. The essential change is this: that in this decade and into the next century, we're no longer the same consumers.

We're consumed out. Many of us are way over our heads in debt as individuals. The national debt, our collective debt, seems hopeless. If we go on living as before, what we'll be consuming is our future, and that of our children's. If we change—scale back, choose more selectively, reverse our priorities from quantity to quality, then, according to Darwin: we'll be fit enough to survive.

Think of the chapters that follow as *business lessons of the future*, showing how the consumer/business world will be changed as the trends change why we buy and what we buy.

These lessons will uncover just how hard it will be to reach the new consumer (but definite ways to do it). They'll talk about the revolution that will signal the end of shopping and advertising, as we know them today. They'll also show how successful marketers can employ strategies that are more human in scale, and more in keeping with the difficult realities ahead. (People will put their money where their morals are.)

The business lessons of the future will show marketers (always a few paces behind), how to catch up to what future consumers want.

And they'll show what action is needed *now* to catch up in time.

Preventive Business:
Your First Line
of Defense

Just before consumers stop doing something, they do it with a vengeance. (Like binging before you start your diet.) That's what we told a client, a credit card company, that believed the flurry of spending activity it was seeing last year was a secure sign for the future. In fact, the opposite was true.

Companies who made money off the fiscal hedonism of the eighties have cause to worry. The consumer world has changed.

Although its business was only slightly off, our client wanted to talk about the future of credit cards. It was still projecting that consumer spending patterns would continue, more or less, as they had—with only an occasional downturn. But, just in case its calculations were wrong, the company wanted to hear about the trends. To be able to consider the future from all angles. Smart.

In fact, what our client was observing was the last binge of stockpiling before the Great Consumer Pullback. Consumers were merely building inventories. And then, abruptly, shopping stopped.

America has entered a phase we're calling "Decession"—recessionary spending with depressionary thinking. The recessionary spending element has come and gone in predictable cycles over the last years. What's new, however, is the depressionary thinking. A bleak change in consumer psychology, like the thirties.

Consumers are holding on to whatever money they have, balancing resources, instead of spending. Gone are the "impulse" buys. Instead of, "That's a great sweater. And I don't have that color;" it's, "I have enough sweaters. I don't need it." Even if things are put on sale, a Decession Consumer simply doesn't want them, at any price.

No buying, no credit carding. As a result, card use could go down significantly over the next few years.

To minimize the downturn and maximize its strengths, our client needed to explore these questions: "How do you put value into the credit system?" "How do you reconcile credit with a Decession sensibility?"

In other words: *How do you restructure a business that depends on consumer spending?*

For the credit business, the answer is in shifting the main emphasis: a re-orientation from company-convenient to consumer-convenient. Instead of being part of the financial ill-health and overextension in America, credit companies should concentrate on taking charge of America's financial wellness. Healing the consumer debt crisis. Stretching the contemporary concept of credit—first, to credit control, then, to credit planning.

How? By providing every consumer with financial services that were once available only to the very wealthy—such as counseling to select smarter investments, higher-rate bank accounts, or more secure retirement plans. The counseling could take place in the cocoon (by phone, fax, computer—or mail) where it's more convenient—and safe.

Credit card companies will have to learn to *compete* for the dollar. By offering incentives. American Express has just come up with an annuity savings plan. It will bill you a specified amount each month, and pay you a substantial 10% interest—for now.

Why couldn't a credit card company also give a preferred rate to a cardholder who wanted to roll over a tax refund into her two-year-old's college education fund? Or to consumers who pay their bills early? (Every little bit helps; the Discover card gives a small cash rebate on purchases at card year's end—up to 10%.)

Preventive Business is the principle at work here. It's coming up with sound business solutions to *prevent* an industry from making strategic miscalculations—or from playing ostrich, as the consumer world changes. Prevention can be accomplished by restructuring the company's product, or simply by diversifying. Taking action before disaster strikes.

—Kodak, by expanding into laser and computer technology, is practicing Preventive Business. If print imaging becomes less important, it will still be in business. And big business—from prints to printers with Ektaplus 7016, which is perfectly positioned for the home office. (The name could be better—Ektaplus sounds too much like Platypus.)

—Estée Lauder, by opening the first Origins store, is starting to provide the consumer with a more convenient, more personalized place to shop than cumbersome department stores.

—Philip Morris, by diversifying and buying Kraft and General Foods, has protected its future profitability. Everyone has to eat.

—Time Warner, Inc., by splintering off into the home video market, is participating in a newer, faster world than magazines.

It's not always easy to practice Preventive Business. To go for the *blockbusters*—only to have them turn into *busts*. But, by following the trends, a company can more easily switch its focus, resurge in new areas.

IBM, as we all know, has built its main business on providing computers for offices. But, astutely, they foresaw that home usage (Cashing Out) would be a large growth area. In response, they created the PS/1, a very friendly product that's much simpler to set up (it has only two plugs). BrainReserve helped position this ready-to-go computer with IBM's Tony Santelli; creating a language (plain English instead of Computerese) and a "hands-on" approach that any computer-ignorant consumer can master.

It's also possible to look around at existing businesses and project their "preventives" for the future.

For example, suppose more and more people are looking for fresh foods only (Staying Alive). Canned soup companies, while understanding the consumers' desire for freshness, would have a hard time delivering a daily or biweekly product (high cost, high spoilage). But a well-thought-out alternative, such as putting the soup into jars (as the French do; better flavor, no metal aftertaste) might be the "prevention." (Sauces would be a natural line extension.)

Or, Federal Express, known for its reliable delivery (but inevitably hurt by the growth of fax) could take their expertise and translate it into home delivery (grocery, discount store)—a service that would pick up an order and quickly bring it to your home.

The Japanese have a cultural intuition for Preventive Business, and for being leap years ahead. Predicting that outside glitz would be antistatus for the '90s, Toyota's newest car has all the luxury on the inside.

These are, in essence, examples that are the reverse of the ostrich principal: holding your corporate head high and out of the sand.

Not being afaid of what's coming is to practice Preventive Business. Bravely, freely. Because Fear of the Future can only lead to Failure.

The 1000#:
Real Help,
Twenty-Four
Hours a Day

The line between selling and service is blurring. Consumers want information and they want it fast.

The toll-free 800 number is an attempt to give consumers speedy answers, easy answers. Corporations today are almost required to have one (not to be left out in the cold). In fairness, some 800 numbers work well—usually those primed to sell. There is a finite amount of commonly asked questions in direct mail, and the operators are usually trained enough to answer them.

Some of the airlines' 800 numbers work well, too, except that during peak traveling hours—the very time when frantic travelers need information fastest—they're busy, busy, busy.

And now there's a push for a personal 800 number—another way of "calling home" even more.

But the original purpose of the 800 number, to help consumers find out answers about a company's product, is too often obscured by 800 inefficiency. Dissatisfied consumers end up more frustrated and angry *after* they've called an 800 number for help.

After reading at length about the Perrier recall, a pregnant friend of mine called a competing company's 800 number to ask whether there was any possible danger in her drinking their mineral water. The 800 operator hadn't even *heard* about Perrier's problems, and had absolutely nothing to say to assuage her caller's fears. End of discussion. End of customer.

The story goes on. My friend then called Perrier's 800 number. The operator of the Perrier Hot Line didn't even know what benzene (the reason for the recall) was or that it was a health hazard. Even worse.

Consumers remember stories like these and swap them with friends. Not good for business.

The '90s is not the time to be careless about the 800 number, the front-line access to your consumer. When it's working right, the 800 number is the best means of disseminating information, expressing a corporate soul. A voice-to-voice way of opening a dialogue with your consumers one-on-one.

All managers should have to work their corporations' 800 numbers. Even the company's top executives should take turns. It's a good education. After a time on the switchboard, they would understand that the 800 number is a valuable *resource,* a direct link with the consumer. Not just an expense to be endured because all your competitors have one.

The 900 numbers seem more attentive, providing better service—probably because the customer pays for the call. Unfortunately, although many are "legit," the 900 series is irrevocably linked to sex and chat lines, and don't really command the consumer's respect.

At BrainReserve, we've been focusing on ways to move on from the 800, the 900, numbers. Looking at ways to turn this technology to better (more time efficient, more human efficient) use.

What we think will be next in numbers is the 1000 number. A number to call that will put an expert on the line to fix your computer, your finances, your kids' problems; even get you legal, medical, or marital advice.

What is it worth? Our research says the consumer would be

willing to pay from $15 to hear how to quick-fix an appliance (cheaper than a service call and more convenient), up to $100 for a family-counseling session with each member on a different phone extension (or a conference call).

The bottom line on the numbers game is that you've got to keep all lines open. When your consumers want help, they want it immediately. Day and night. Weekdays and weekends (whose VCR ever got jammed between 9 and 5, Monday through Friday?) And they're willing to pay for the privilege.

There's gold in them 'thar numbers.

You can weigh it in consumer loyalty.

Hot-Branding

When everyone wants something, there's a reason.

If in the past few years we've gained quality, we've done so at a cost: We've lost style.

The next wave will be style, and style with a vengeance. It'll be a reaction to the fact that the differences have been leeched out of everything. I call it Hot-Branding: Penetrating the fortress with style, yet keeping quality and function intact. It's not about being marked by designer initials, but by a deeper "branding": character, style, eccentricity. Hot-Branding also has to do with personality—being kicky, whimsical, different, odd, honest.

And how do you achieve it? By adding color, spirit, soul, life, and fun. Maybe a tinge of irony. By going back to study the stylish forties, fifties, and sixties, and infusing your product with a new/old charisma. By actively fighting against bland, boxy, and boring.

As consumers, we're blanded out. Too many things that we think are good for us to eat are white—white chicken, white fish, white wine, all those clear mineral waters.

And if almost everything we should eat is white, almost everything we now drive is boring.

Cars used to come in all shapes, instantly identifiable: the two-seater Thunderbird, the winged Cadillac, the pointy Torino, the frisky Mustang. But then, the expensive European cars got boxy and boring. Then, Japanese cars imitated that look. Now most cars are look-alikes. Except for the Mazda Miata; rounded like an old, bathtub Porsche: a Wandering Cocoon within the price range of Small Indulgences; a safe Fantasy Adventure for the Vigilante Consumer with high standards. You know what it is the minute you see it; you know how much it costs; you know the four colors it comes in. Hot-Branding accentuates the recognition factor. It's fun.

- The Gap is Hot-Branding. When you walk into the Gap, any Gap, you're surrounded by it; it's a total experience. Simple, functional, inexpensive. It offers variety and a sense of immersion—when you're there, you're there. You're doing the Gap.
- Ralph Lauren's Country Store is Hot-Branding. When you walk in, you enter a world of antique paintings, country crafts, twig tables, hook rugs, and Native American jewelry that provides a historical backdrop to the casual but elegant clothes. It looks and feels authentic because they had an authentic American folklorist, Ben Apfelbaum, on staff. The store is real, functional, and very expensive. Hot-Branding is priceless.
- Rainforest Crunch is Hot-Branding. Ben & Jerry's candy with a social conscience, because the cashew and Brazil nuts come from the Amazon Basin. Buying from the tropical forest preserves the tropical forest (40% of the profits go back into the rainforest economy; 20% for peace). You're doing good while you're eating something indescribably good.
- Nike is Hot-Branding, because these tough sports shoes have become a symbol for America's need for a nudge. A reminder to be good. Positive reinforcement. Athletes-as-heroes are

encouraging our wayward youth to "Just Do It."

- Origins is Hot-Branding. A simple line of cosmetics (from Lauder) that do more than make you look good. They make you feel good—inside and out. The best-seller is a small bottle of lotion called "Peace of Mind." Just rub it on your temples and rub out your stress.
- Nikon is Hot-Branding. It's the professional photographer's camera. Advanced, technologically perfect, and comfortingly classic. It works. Always has, always will.

It may be that Hot-Branding is something you have to feel first. It may be that, as with jazz, either you just feel it in your soul—or you never get it. In any case, there's room for at least one Hot-Branded product in every category. The trends can get you branded. And that's how to insure your future.

Ask Not What Your Consumer Can Do for You, but What You Can Do for Your Consumer

The *key* to making the '90s work for you will depend on how able you are to forget your old tricks—and learn the new ways of this decade.

Perfect packaging, beautiful product shots, cleverness, style over substance, or hype just won't work anymore.

The *key* to your consumer will depend on how much extra you can actually deliver. Product, plus, plus, plus. Such as discounts to reward loyal customers or giving part of your profits to a community project.

*Your consumer databank will become your most vital resource. Companies will set up new departments devoted to finding ways of opening dialogues with consumers, and keeping them going. Even the vague term "consumers" will be obsolete: you'll call them by *name*.

Let's say you sell microwave ovens. A new customer comes in and buys one for her apartment. Learn her name and mail her a completed warranty/guarantee (why make her fill out the form), along with a new microwave cookbook. You should be ready with a 900#, so your purchasers can call in with any questions they may have, from timing to meal planning.

*Life will be easier for the consumer when marketers work together more effectively to penetrate the Cocoon. Cross-marketing can be a huge business.

Let's say you own a nursery, and you sell a new home owner some perennials, bulbs, and evergreen trees.

Within days, you've passed on that consumer's name, and the fledgling gardener receives several samples (peat moss, standard fertilizer) from the hardware store, brochures showing outdoor furniture, work clothing, and garden ornaments, along with an invitation to a meeting at the local garden club.

Buying, selling, and using names will become a much nicer and more sophisticated industry than it is today. Every new consumer will be pinpointed, targeted, and courted by piggyback marketers.

The strategy is like the old-fashioned concept of the Welcome Wagon, where new residents were given little "gifts" and offered special rates to try all the local merchants. The "cooperative" approach recognizes that buying one item should lead to buying a *chain* of items.

Consumers might even offer to give their names to such mega-companies as Philip Morris (owner of Kraft General Foods and Miller Brewing) who produce a wide range of products in exchange for ongoing home delivery.

*You can penetrate the Cocoon with personalized service. The more you're willing to *help* the consumer, the more accessible she'll be.

If your business is in selling major household goods—appliances, home entertainment—try launching a "preventive care" program. Why wait until the washing machine breaks? A tune-up and cleaning of all appliances every nine months can keep things in optimum running order. What's in it for you? Faithful consumers; and a chance to "presell"—advising the customers ahead of time what's coming next. If they believe in your service, they'll buy your product.

Ask yourself what you can do to earn the loyalty of your consumers. And, then, deliver. You'll have earned their allegiance for life.

FoodFutures

"You are what you eat" is often heard in our halls, because to us, observing "the way we eat" is tantamount to a consumer's true confessions.

We maintain that trends most often have their genesis in eating habits. Because we all eat. We all talk about it. Compared with buying durable goods, eating is relatively inexpensive, an easy way to try something new or different. From a consumer's standpoint, there's always another snack, another meal that's no more than a few hours away. A bad food investment is only a small loss.

One of the best ways to track trends is to track food. Any new food information sets off our trend alarm at BrainReserve to watch if an early indication could foreshadow a larger cultural swing. For example, food shifts have signaled several of the current trends:

*One of the first hints of Cocooning was in the sudden decline in restaurant business in the major cities. Where were the patrons? Holing up at home. They were nestled in their nooks eating take-out food or ordering in, nibbling popcorn and watching movies on the VCR.

*Restaurants featuring Thai, Vietnamese, and other Oriental cuisines, or those hot tropical restaurants with Caribbean food and drinks, were, to us, among the early signs that people were looking for safe escape in Fantasy Adventure.

*An early Small Indulgence we cited was the Dove Bar, an instant, yet premium, gratification. This "I Deserve It" syndrome became one of the fastest-growing trends we'd ever tracked.

*Someone in the office noticed an article about a gourmet picnic, with a trendy sun-dried tomato and pasta salad as the entrée. The dessert: Oreos, the perfect cookie for the child in us, for Down-Aging grown-ups.

It's also an interesting exercise to review the recent chapters of consumer history, then project the future, through food. Just think back to the insular fifties, when the most exotic foods imaginable were egg rolls and mushy chop suey from the one nearby Chinese restaurant; or possibly a heavy beef bourguignon prepared by an adventurous friend.

Then came the plastic, the tasteless era: the fast food and frozen food of the sixties.

In the seventies, American food was simple. We were still in awe of the European cuisines. Yet, the marketers' rule of thumb was that Americans wouldn't buy it (here) if they couldn't pronounce it (from over there).

By the global-village eighties, however, croissants (pronounced "cross-ants" or any which way) had become a $500 million business. Menus were suddenly international mix-and-match: Chino/ Latino restaurants, mini-pizzas sprinkled with French goat cheese, Japanese sushi, Mexican salsas.

By the late eighties and early nineties, meat loaf and mashed potatoes were back "in" in America. We were seeing a rerun of the '50s with Diner Nostalgia. Also, Bistro food, the best roast chicken, the crispiest french fries. Beans and grains and polenta. That's why we were so excited when Simon & Schuster's Charlie

Hayward and Jack McKeown retained us to help launch *The Family Circle Cookbook*, a general teach-America-the-new-way-to-cook book. (The new way meaning quick, healthful and making use of ethnic ingredients in classic recipes.)

And the next chapter?

Egonomics hasn't hit the food arena yet—but it will. Customized food will be next. It will be recognized that your body's nutritional needs are different from your husband's. You'll be serving meals for mood—to reduce stress, enhance energy, induce sleep. A certain bread to quiet you; a special beef to stimulate you. Foods by age, by stage of life—teen menus, menopause meals. Traditional/medicinals—to aid breathing, to boost you when you're nursing or have PMS.

Serious foods. Survival foods. Healing foods. Soon to be available for you and your family.

ConsumerSpeak

If you want to know what consumers want, ask. That's the foundation of consumer research, and that's where true wisdom lies. The trick, of course, is knowing what questions to ask. And knowing how to listen to the answers. Because the answers come in another language. A language that is a combination of shy forthrightness and eager-to-pleasedness; "good citizen" polite behavior and unconscious, brutal honesty. I call it ConsumerSpeak.

ConsumerSpeak is a language you hear in very special situations—in Focus Group rooms and Mall Intercepts, in One-on-Ones and In-Depth Interviews—in all of those "situational formats" which marketing research people have devised to help marketers "talk" to consumers.

Let me back up. If you are a marketer, this vocabulary is probably painfully familiar to you. If you are a consumer, we'll let you in on the secret. Consumer research *is* an amazing process. And filled with astonishing James Bond-movie trappings, like two-way mirrors, sensitive microphones, and almost-psychic "leaders" who know how to tap into the group's real motivations and feelings— à la group therapy. In the extreme, there are even techniques for testing television commercials that involve electrodes to measure the heartbeat and palm sweat of viewing consumers, or dials consumers turn as their interest rises and falls.

But here's the heart of the matter: marketers need to know what consumers have to say. The simpler the format is, the better it works. Focus Groups—where eight or so specially screened consumers come together to *talk* about a product or an idea— usually build to a crescendo with a handful of rowdy talkers and always one quiet type. Or Triads—a more intense group of three. We especially like In-Depth Interviews—one-on-one conversations with consumers. It's a more intimate process, more probing. You can reach a deep level of understanding about a consumer's likes and dislikes.

What's the key to understanding ConsumerSpeak? Just remember that all the participants are trying to act civilized. To play the social game successfully. Since our first toddling steps to socialization, we have been taught to be nice, to say only nice things, to make the other person feel comfortable, not to shock or make waves (this especially applies to women). Even more: to give the right answers to the questions. ("What does the teacher want me to say?" "What will make me look good?") This is, of course, an admirable social phenomenon. But it can destroy honest communication, unless you're aware that it's going on.

Consumers mostly say what they think you *want* to hear. What they think their *role* is to say (if they're pegged as mothers or lawyers or outdoor adventurers). What they think will not hurt your feelings. What they think will make them seem smarter or nicer or healthier than the last person who spoke (of course, no one ever admits to eating a whole quart of ice cream). Anything but the absolute truth.

Unless you know how to translate ConsumerSpeak. For example, when you have just presented an idea for what you hope is a crackerjack new product, here's the difference between what the consumer says and what she means.

WHAT THE CONSUMER SAYS:	"That would make a great gift."
WHAT THE CONSUMER MEANS:	"I wouldn't have that in my house."
WHAT THE CONSUMER SAYS:	"My sister would love it."
WHAT THE CONSUMER MEANS:	"I myself hate it."
WHAT THE CONSUMER SAYS:	"That would be great for camping."
WHAT THE CONSUMER MEANS:	"Boy, is that a useless object."
WHAT THE CONSUMER SAYS:	"My husband would love it, but my kids wouldn't like it at all."
WHAT THE CONSUMER MEANS:	"It'd probably be okay once, but I rarely do/cook/make things separately for my husband and kids. Who has time for it?"
WHAT THE CONSUMER SAYS:	"I guess an electric dust-ball magnet for under the bed *would* make the house cleaner, but is it hard to use?"
WHAT THE CONSUMER MEANS:	"Give me a break."
WHAT THE CONSUMER SAYS:	"It'd be great for entertaining."
WHAT THE CONSUMER MEANS:	"This has nothing to do with my real life."
WHAT THE CONSUMER SAYS:	"That'd be a nice switch from macaroni and cheese."
WHAT THE CONSUMER MEANS:	"Everybody loves macaroni and cheese. It's easy; I make it once a week and it's the only time nobody complains about the food. Why should I switch?"
WHAT THE CONSUMER SAYS:	"Oh, I always have one of those in the cupboard."
WHAT THE CONSUMER MEANS:	"I bought one once and I think it's still in the cupboard, probably pretty dusty by now."
WHAT THE CONSUMER SAYS:	"I like it because it's 'natural.' "
WHAT THE CONSUMER MEANS:	"Natural is boring, but I'm not going to say so."

WHAT THE CONSUMER SAYS: "That might be a good idea for special occasions."

WHAT THE CONSUMER MEANS: "I'll never use it, but I don't want to hurt your feelings."

Here are four ConsumerSpeak insights we keep in mind when we listen to people talk to us about products.

The "On Hand" Rejection. If the consumer says it would be great to keep "on hand" in the cupboard, closet, garage, freezer, car trunk, basement (you get the picture), she is pushing the product away with *both* hands. (The flip-side: if she volunteers what she would get *rid* of to make room for the new idea, that's a directionally enthusiastic response.) Occasionally, we make "cabinet checks," where we boldly go into a consumer's home to peer into the pantry, the fridge—and spot-check what products are *actually* there.

The God-Said-I-Should Acceptance. If the product/idea you are presenting represents a "should" behavior (a hot breakfast meal for the kids that takes a while to make, for example, or almost anything relating to "good mother" behavior or "natural goodness"), then the big initial enthusiasm is usually guilt-provoked. The enthusiasm can often be false. Counter it by saying, "I know you want to give the kids a hot breakfast every morning, but isn't it hard, when you yourself have to rush around getting ready for work?" If enthusiasm continues (without *too* much defensiveness), you may be onto something.

The Action vs. Intention Differential. Learn to distinguish real actions from intentions. Does she *really* floss three times a day, or does she just want to? Would she really go out and buy your product on the way home, or does she just "intend" to. Where's the urgency? (The flip-side of this, of course, is the "negative expressed intention"—"I would *never* pay good money for that"— followed by a secret positive action. Like the woman who rejected a demo product we once showed in a Focus Group, then secretly asked the moderator if she could take it home.)

The Too-Soon-to-Ask Rejection. If the idea is on-trend for the future, the consumer won't know yet whether she'll want it or not. Be cautious about taking her rejection too seriously. Instead, listen for "creative builds" on the idea, or listen to how she associates the new idea with other things in her life right now: a great source of future usage clues. Five years ago, a gadget for bundling newspapers for recycling wouldn't have interested her. Today, it does.

What we're really saying is "Let's communicate." Ongoing consumer dialogue is essential, and the more we all retreat into our armored cocoons, the more essential it will become.

At BrainReserve, we conduct thousands of consumer interviews every year. We talk to people about products, of course, and business ideas. But we also talk to them about their lives, their expectations, their fantasies, and their disappointments— how their lives have changed in the last five years, and what they hope will happen over the next ten or twenty.

Being able to hear what the consumer is saying is the foundation of our trends. And, if the truth be known, it's the foundation of the future.

How to Tell
ConsumerTime

Just as ConsumerSpeak is a language unto itself, so ConsumerTime is a timeline unto itself. To read it correctly you have to adjust your clock dramatically: to future time. It isn't here yet, but it's coming. And you had better be ready when it arrives.

Telling ConsumerTime is the way you determine when your product is going to say to the consumer: "Now!"

It's what some of my clients have called a "leap of faith"—concentrating their efforts on what is still an unseen future. ("I just can't see a world," someone once told me, "where red-blooded American men will be eating yogurt or drinking lite beer." But *that* someone obviously didn't know about the trend Staying Alive.)

When you consider the unavoidable time lag involved in marketing (it takes most companies 18 to 24 months to launch a new product, 9 months to a year to bring a new positioning to the airwaves)—it becomes clear that the *only* way to look at time is fast-forward. What consumers tell you they want "right this minute" is not necessarily what they will want with the most urgency 12 months or 2 years down the road.

So you make that leap into future time on the basis of trends: TrendTime is long-term time, (a trend has a life span of at least 10 years; Cocooning is evolving into its second decade). Trends are the most accurate way (we know) of predicting what ConsumerTime in the marketplace will ultimately be. Apply the trends now, and your product or positioning will be smack on target when the consumer catches up with it. *Don't* apply the trends now, and someone else will beat you to it. And it will be too late for you to catch up.

Fine-tuning your timeline, in sync with the trends, requires that you be aware of another occurrence we call Time Elasticity. It's the phenomena of ConsumerTime slowing down, speeding up, even briefly stopping, in response to outside events, or even to the trends themselves.

When war was declared, say, and people burrowed deeper into their cocoons. Fine, that was in keeping with the Cocooning trend (no major shifting). But ConsumerTime stopped momentarily. You saw a blip on the timeline, caused by a cataclysmic event. But think back to when the recent war ended and people took to the streets, celebrating. Did you abandon your trend-wise product or positioning? No. Because the timeline continues. People will evenually see what *else* is wrong out in the streets, out in the world. And they'll head back to their cocoons. The trends will remain intact.

The trends themselves can make ConsumerTime speed up or slow down. As the Acceleration Syndrome built to its peak (giving birth to 99 Lives)—we saw ConsumerTime get faster and faster. But, time, in this decade, will be slowing down more. We will adopt a sort of "Slow is Beautiful" motif. It's a reaction against the high velocity of the '80s, an impulse to Cash Out for a better life. We're an aging (if Down-Aging) population, and we'll be slowing down, maybe whiling away an afternoon, maybe taking extra time to carefully compose a fax, the way people used to carefully compose a letter. Slow will be the cultural backdrop of this decade.

At the same time, ConsumerTime can speed up from exterior

marketing pressure. Sheer market competition forces *everyone* future-forward. If you don't get to market fast enough, the Japanese will, or the Germans, or the people who have Cashed Out and are willing to work all day, all night, and every weekend till it's done. In a global economy, where we can't predict who's going to supersede the Japanese, the Germans, or some as-yet-unrevealed major player, marketing time has to be on fast-forward, even in a decade where, otherwise, slow and steady wins the race.

Be aware of Time Elasticity, but don't be thrown off by it. (Think of it as one of those watches that shows three different time zones at once.)

Don't lose sight of the fact that the *time* you're on is TrendTime.

It's the surest guide to ConsumerTime and the securest guide to the future.

THE NEW MARKETING FRONTIER

The future waits for no man. No woman. No company.

Marketing the Corporate Soul

It used to be enough just to make a fairly decent product and market it. Not anymore. In the '90s, you've got to have a Corporate Soul. The consumer will want to know who you are before buying what you sell. And who you are isn't always an easy question to answer. Who you are will mean publicly stating your environmental policy, your stance on health care and child care, how (or if) you deal with an apartheid country, what other brands you have or other names you market under.

More importantly, activist groups today are busy unearthing corporate attitudes. A feminist group, Media Watch, has targeted Guess Jeans, among others, for its perceived sexist advertising. Pro-choice and pro-lifers squared off against AT&T's decision to end its donations to Planned Parenthood. It's those kinds of policies that hurt a company's image; when things are not all they seem. In a small way, I can remember when people I knew, sophisticated business people, felt almost betrayed to discover that

Pepperidge Farm (folksy, homemade image) and Godiva Chocolates (upscale, precious) were owned by Campbell's (corporate, mass-produced).

The corporation, in trying to edge closer to its consumer, has to remember that we've learned our lesson well: "Don't open the doors to strangers." We'll want to know in advance who's trying to gain entry into our cocoon. But we'll be likelier to let you in if we can respect your Corporate Soul.

The general direction corporations have taken over the past decade has been to retreat behind their products, leaving them to speak, in effect, for themselves. Promoting products over their makers.

What corporations need to do next is form relationships with their consumers. Relationships based on trust. And what inspires trust? Decency. Corporations that *do* good, that *are* good, will inspire trust. They'll find easy access to the cocoon.

The Decency Positioning is still up for grabs in almost every category. Shocking but true: the Decency Positioning is still one of the hardest to convince corporations to adopt: it's tough to deliver. But it only takes one company with a Corporate Soul doing the right thing to pull ahead in each category.

Like *Good Housekeeping*, in magazines. The seven sisters (*Ladies Home Journal* to *McCall's*) were having a hard time (late '80s). Their images were blurred. It was getting increasingly difficult to get advertisers to buy pages between their covers. *Good Housekeeping* hired BrainReserve to help.

Our initial analysis showed that it already had a Corporate Soul (only it wasn't always top of mind). Virtually all products advertised in the magazine are covered by *Good Housekeeping*'s "Consumers' Policy," which offers replacement or refund of the purchase price if the product proves defective.

Based on its ethics, we saw that the magazine had an opportunity to be positioned as the social conscience of the '90s,: The Decency Decade. The announcement ran on January 2, 1990, in the *New York Times* and *The Wall Street Journal*. It read, "The Decency Decade Has Begun. *Good Housekeeping* Is Its Voice." The text explained that *Good Housekeeping*, as a consumer authority, would stand behind its seal; would establish a Department of Chemistry and Environmental Studies in the institute;

and would run an ongoing earth watch feature called "Green Watch." The magazine also created "Green Watch Awards" to honor those making significant contributions to the improvement of the environment. In other words, *Good Housekeeping* made a commitment to wear its Corporate Soul on its corporate sleeve. The pledge to Decency was strong and powerful. Ad pages went up. "Good House" is the only one of the seven sisters to show a gain that year.

Rubbermaid, Inc. was one of the first companies we worked with to grasp the decency sell; it had been doing it instinctively all along—great company, great products, great name recognition, great employee morale. It was named #2 in *Fortune*'s list of America's top 306 companies. At the turn of this decade, however, Rubbermaid was intuitive enough to see itself as being in the center of the "eco-marketplace." It was linked in the public's mind with recycling, the important concerns of sorting and storing.

What Rubbermaid clearly needed was a meaningful environmental platform to separate it from the crowded, cynical claims of today's eco-marketplace. It needed, to put it another way, not only to advertise its products but to advertise itself.

Under a "Rubbermaid and You: Helping the Earth Bounce Back" umbrella, we worked with the company to position itself for the years ahead. The "Rubbermaid and You" element in the slogan was key. Consumers, we found, feel hopeless and alone in their recycling efforts. Rubbermaid had to replace this hopelessness with optimism; form a partnership, a community with the consumer (under the guise of "together we can help the earth bounce back"); and place itself at the forefront of the emerging environmental arena.

In our final report, we presented Rubbermaid with a list of potential new products to exemplify its environmental awareness (i.e., a system that holds returnables; fits in both your car trunk and a shopping cart). And we devised simple ways of broadcasting Corporate Soul. For instance, a sticker could be designed for all its products with a recycling symbol on it or we even suggested using an image of its president, Wolf Schmitt (handsome; corporately responsible). Included also was a "wish list," drawn from one of our BrainJams, of twenty actionable product and packaging ideas—such as "Return this product to us for recycling/get a discount on your next purchase"—to implement over the next few years. It may take a while to improve the earth, but Rubbermaid has shown its heart is in the right place.

Other companies could take some first steps. By proclaiming their Corporate Soul on myriad corporate seals, an instant stamp for the consumer to see. By revealing cradle-to-grave biographies of all their products. By allowing full disclosure, nothing secret, nothing hidden.

You can't fake a Corporate Soul; either you have one or you'd better create one, fast. Depending on your industry, the Decency Decade demands that you send out a loud-and-clear message (a Corporate Promise) that goes something like this:

For heavy industries: "Our industry as a whole has made some real mistakes, some we knew about and now regret, some we couldn't have foreseen. Here's what our company is doing to rectify them." For instance, if Exxon's Chairman, Lawrence G. Rawl, had handled the *Valdez* spill by telling the American public this message (the way Jim Burke did during the Tylenol crisis), consumers might have been forgiving, instead of harboring anger for the company. Although only 10,000 customers cut up their charge cards, the company's name has been stained (as black as the oil).

· *For service industries:* "With so many social problems (crime, illiteracy, disease, etc.) plaguing us today, our company wants to help out more. Here's the way we thought we could do the most good." The fashion and design industry has pitched in to raise funds for AIDS research (DIFFA—Design Industries Foundation for AIDS—is one of the mainstays of that movement). McDonald's instituted a network of Ronald McDonald Houses, and promotes a McSeniors plan to employ the elderly as well as a McJobs program for the handicapped. The Burger King Academy is an alternative high school for unmotivated students and dropouts.

For packaged goods companies: "For years, we've been packaging our products to get your attention. Now we're recycling to help save the earth." Kodak has focused on plans to recycle its film canisters (7.5 million tons of plastic each year). Procter & Gamble has started a program to recycle diapers. Both Coke and Pepsi are using recycled plastic bottles for their sodas.

For regulated industries: "As part of the liquor industry, we believe in drinking in moderation. Our company recognizes that liquor, if abused, is a dangerous substance." Seagram's provides a parent's handbook to help families discuss the ramifications of alcohol consumption. Anheuser-Busch budgeted $35 million for an alcohol awareness and education campaign. Miller Brewing has come up with a "Think When You Drink" ad campaign. Or for the tobacco industry: "We believe in your right to smoke, if you choose. But we also believe in your right to quit." Nothing's been done yet, but the industry someday may research revolutionary new ways to help you modify your behavior . . . should you desire to do so.

These are the four steps that companies can follow to find a Corporate Soul and win the consumer's heart in the '90s:

*Acknowledgment. Our industry hasn't always done everything in its power to make the world a better place.

*Disclosure. This is who we were. And this is the company we're trying, with your help, to become.

*Accountability. Here is *how* we define our arena of responsibility, and *who* can be held accountable.

*Presentation. Here is what we pledge to you, the consumer: you'll find our Corporate Soul in all our products.

The corporate world will have to change its priorities, and reward different strengths. The status that an M.B.A. held for marketers in the '80s will be replaced by the status of a new M.B.S. (Master of Business Soul). Guaranteed to be good through the year 2000. And beyond.

The End of Shopping

In Orwell's classic *1984*, the state controlled the screen. In the year 2000, the consumer will control the screen. The computerized shopping screen.

The home cocoon will be the site of the future shopping center. All members of the family will be able to shop from one location. Instead of going to the store, the store will come to us, no matter how unusual the product or how frequently needed. On our screens, we'll be able to hear about the latest new products or styles, or order up our old favorites.

Like the corporation, the shopping experience as we know it, has grown cumbersome, inefficient, a violation of the trends. The big department stores are discovering that it's no longer possible to be all things to all customers. The shopping center is becoming a dinosaur in the grand scheme of things.

Today's mail-order catalogs and sale fliers (piled up in the house somewhere waiting to be thumbed through and discarded) are obsolete—too much wasted paper; plus the post office is too inefficient, postage too expensive, to keep sending them through the mail.

The means of distribution will be the next consumer-oriented revolution. Direct shopping from the producer to you—bypassing the retailer altogether, no middlemen, no stops along the way.

Home delivery will become, not an extra service, but a way of life. One truck delivering to a hundred customers will be a much more efficient use of resources than a hundred customers driving to stores. There will be holding tanks in your house for milk, soda, mineral water (all refrigerated), and bins for laundry soap and dog kibble, for example, all delivered like home heating oil.

Once home distribution takes hold, stores will gradually become obsolete. For big-ticket items—media centers, cars, home furnishing and decoration—sales reps will come to the home. For food items and packaged goods, delivered samples will replace shopping-and-trying. For new or novelty or impulse items, there will be portable showrooms, like Good Humor trucks for grown-ups (we'll run outside to shop when we hear the bell . . .).

Packaging is over. Frequent dialogue between manufacturer and consumer, as well as heightened brand loyalty, will eliminate the need for any complicated packaging. Consumers will give manufacturers their feedback through computer 800 numbers. And manufacturers will keep a panel of consumers on call to look at, test, and evaluate any new or revised product ideas. (It would be a smart move to involve consumers early in a product's development phase, giving them a vested interest in its success— and giving manufacturers a chance to hear "real" comments from "real" customers.)

The actual future shopping experience will be streamlined by such innovations as these:

AdverNews. Looking at a screen each morning, the reader can "browse" through news headlines and listings of ads and coupons. After indicating what one wants to read in depth, a printer prints out a customized newspaper. Much less paper to recycle. At the end of the month, the reader gets billed only for what's been printed out. And companies placing the ads are charged by how many readers elected to print out their information. Plus, they'll receive an index of the names/addresses/demographics of their targeted readers.

ScreenMail. All day long the mail comes in, visualized on the screen or printed out—it's how we shop, pay bills, organize incoming information, and send our own information out. There are specials, such as "One-Day" ScreenMail Offers, much like the old-fashioned One-Day Sales. With mail-order catalogs obsolete, ScreenMail ordering is thriving.

Before ordering clothes, the consumer superimposes his/her own image on the screen to "try" things on and see how the styles and colors will actually look (quite an advancement over tracing your foot on paper to order shoes from the L.L. Bean catalog.) Apparel companies will offer custom sizing, tailoring, and color selections suited to the buyer's preferences, as well as special accessories that will finish "dressing" the customer's look.

InfoBuying. What are the three best cars on the market for long-term maintenance? The three easiest-to-use VCR's? The nearest places to buy them at the lowest price? Ask the InfoBank in your computer for the answer. Then you can make your decision from the screen and computer-order your choice at once. (The end of advertising as we know it.)

Two kinds of going-out-to-shop experiences will remain:

1. Specialty boutiques, selling such items as gourmet foods or household and personal products. These small, local, "edited" markets offer personal service. What entices you to buy at these shops (rather than by screen) is also the personality and style of the owners. With so many aspects of shopping now automatic and perfunctory, what remains will have to provide shoppers with a joyful, satisfying experience on an individual basis.

2. Or huge emporiums, where shopping becomes theater.

Filled with dazzling displays, free samples, and unusual bargains, these new emporiums will tempt shoppers by merging the atmosphere of department stores/malls with a three-ring circus. It takes more than just merchandise to bring people out of their Cocoons. They'll come out with their families for the *entertain-*

ment value; shopping will seem like visiting Las Vegas or Disney World. Stores will be run by merchandising impressarios hired to attract consumer attention. Trained instructors will demonstrate new technology and equipment. Ex-Olympian athletes will show off new exercise machines. Chefs will create original recipes using new combinations of food products, pulling people in with the aromas of cooking and samples to taste.

Shopping is an activity we'll plan on doing two or three times a month, as an alternative to the movies or sporting events.

Consuming is what we'll still be doing every day. On screen or off. The end of today's way of shopping is just the beginning of a new way of consumering. Efficient, smart, personable, profitable.

Truth in Advertising

It seemed to me that, in the sixties, advertising was the most creative business around. The consumer world was new, wide open; ads were all creativity, no research. I loved the business when I started in it. I was twenty and I had seen *Pillow Talk* one too many times.

You could feel that consumer world narrowing in the seventies and eighties. Heavy earnest research weighed down ads with somber (and often meaningless) promises—and clients would only buy ads that scored well. The consumer world was quantified.

In the nineties, consumers don't believe the promises anymore. If the ad says "ninety-out-of-a-hundred people prefer *fill-in-the-blank*," we cynically assume that those 90 are the advertiser's 90 best friends and relatives. We know that numbers can be interpreted to mean almost anything. So, the situation now is that numbers have lost their credibility, and yet creativity isn't strong enough to stand on its own. Many of the truly creative people aren't going into advertising these days, choosing to become entrepreneurs instead.

Prior to starting BrainReserve, I used to mull over different ideas with Marty Smith, my "futuristic" boss at the agency. One of our favorite topics was ways to make the "ad biz" pure and noble. Then, when Stuart Pittman and I left to form our own company, we considered acting upon one such lofty idea—and thought about calling it Truth in Advertising. The idea was that we'd advertise only the *best*—the best orange juice, the best car, the best detergent. We would become known for telling the truth. The truth idea was too early for 1974; consumers hadn't burned out yet on hype and novelty (plus we didn't have the backing needed to set up the required product testing facilities).

By now, in the '90s, we're burned out and brusied up enough to hear the truth. Truth in Advertising. A whole new business with someone like a Ralph Nader as CEO. Finally, ads and commercials so truthful that you can believe every word that is written. The Truth in Advertising agency will even sign off on them— and be held accountable for the claims.

Alliances will shift. The traditional partnership has been client and agency merging forces to seduce the consumer. For advertisers to survive in the years to come, they'll have to switch allegiances and change over to the consumer's side. The new partnership will be agency and consumer joining together to glean the truth from the client.

Truth will penetrate the Cocoon.

One single agency may handle all the top three brands in a category. A commercial might say, "Independent studies conducted have shown that companies A, B, and C make the first- second- and third-best vacuum cleaners. Here's how A is better than B and what B has over C and A." It might be that vacuum cleaners A, B, and C will be distinguished by price or features. Consumers will have to decide which variables are important. They'll be given all the information necessary to make a sensible—no hype—focused decision. The approach is like a streamlined *Consumer Reports*. And clients will still pay to make it happen.

There will also be Truth in Advertising commercials on computer shopping screens (in public places or at home). Consumers will punch in what they need to know about what they're hoping to buy. These screens will respond by presenting all the necessary information, again recommending the top three products in the category as well as where they can be purchased.

Interestingly, there's a new beauty magazine called *Allure*, that's based on this very premise. It promises to tell the *truth* about beauty claims, pricing and packaging. Cosmetic companies, as well as the advertisers, will have to respond responsibly.

So Truth in Advertising will change more than one industry. The new advertising will be positioned for the informational benefit of the consumer.

If Truth in Advertising sounds too bare, too spare, too honest, for American companies today, understand that it will be here tomorrow. The consumer has finally peeled off the glitz and grime of the '80s and is ready to hear the truth—to buy the truth, whether business is ready or not.

Breaking the
Age Barrier

It's a fact that our population is aging, that the oldest of the huge baby-boom generation will turn fifty in 1996. It's also true that an aging population is a slippery bunch; hard for marketers to handle.

Some of these fifty-year-olds will be marathon runners. Others will be out of shape and aging fast.

Some will have grown children; others will be parents of toddlers. Some empty-nest mothers will be starting careers for the first time. Other parents will be switching jobs, Cashing Out, or changing identities—with new marriages, residences, bodies or face-lifts.

None of these will remotely resemble the fifty-year-olds that marketers have in their minds' eyes, because fifty doesn't mean what it used to. We're "aging" at different physical/psychological rates than our parents (or grandparents) did. A Down-Aging fifty-year-old, today, looks *young*.

We look this good not only from vanity, from increased life expectancy, or from the pressures of living in a youth-oriented culture—but because most of us can't *afford* to feel fifty. Times are tough; it's not possible to slow down. Baby-boomers, even the oldest ones, have a long way to go before thinking about switching life-cycle gears.

Still, realities are realities, and few of us, for all we do to Stay Alive, can jump as high or look as untouched at fifty as we need to. Products that ease the strain, erase the pain, without labeling themselves as such, will earn a place in this marketplace.

To gain the loyalty of this group, you'll have to find the right "age standard" for your products. Understand first that this aging market actually "feels" about thirty-five. A recent study found that when the majority of fifty-year-olds look into the mirror, they readjust the image and see themselves at about thirty-five. The best way to reach this older consumer then is to find his/her essential thirty-five-year-old self—the one that's vibrant, sexy, fun, still full of hope and possibilities.

Case in point: a large pharmaceutical company retained BrainReserve to analyze why a shampoo they had launched for the fifty-plus market was failing miserably, even though it was an excellent product. The advertising showed a handsome retired couple, walking hand in hand through a garden of Italian statues; then a product shot with a label saying the name and the target, "For 50 +."

Problem one: identification.

You don't want to be confronted everyday by your age on the shower shelf. The women we interviewed resented the fact that a shampoo would give their age away.

Problem two: imagery.

When asked to free-associate, the women thought the statuary made the garden look like a graveyard.

One has to market to the *needs* of the fifty-year-old, not to the *age*. Maybe formulating a shampoo that treats very dry hair (a usual condition for fifty-plus). Make that product with an easier-to-open spout and bigger, bolder print for instructions.

If you break the age barrier, you'll find that a great product subtly geared for an older market will become the norm for many markets. Any product that's comfortable for, accessible to, and usable by an older market should be one that's comfortable for, accessible to, and usable by others (unless it's geriatric-specific, like Depend).

Following this lead, you won't be tempted to market mainstream cosmetics with a separate line of face creams and foundations showing the "mature" woman. Your mainstream line of cosmetics should be targeted to anyone with dry skin.

So, invent a "New Age Herbal Geritol" with younger people on the label.

Fill Pop-Tarts with prunes.

And stop featuring wizened ninety-year-olds as the fifty-plus grandparents of an infant.

Keep the age standard centered on fifty—but fifty going on thirty-five. Terrific. And vital.

Gloria Steinem once remarked, at being told that she looked so young at fifty, "*This* is what fifty looks like."

Cashing in on the Children's Crusade

Just as the '60s brought us the Peaceniks; the '70s, Flower Power; the '80s, Glitz and Greed; the '90s will introduce the Children's Crusade: little ones reshaping our foreign policy, changing our views on education, and saving our environment.

Don't underestimate them, or like Bumble Bee, pay a price. In their case, being part of the tuna boycott. The use of gill nets that ensnared hapless dolphins especially caught the conscience of American schoolchildren. They stopped eating tunafish. And their parents stopped buying it.

Here was a clear case of how the Children's Crusade flexed its growing muscles and wielded its influence over the family-purchasing decisions. But kids also have purchasing power of their own (the so-called "Brat Market" of four to twelve-year-olds is responsible for going through an estimated $75 billion in loose change). According to *Forbes*, big bucks are being spent on the latest videogames (about $20 billion worth) and the thirty-two-year-old Barbie (who wears designer gowns costing over $100). Tapping into this market with its disarmingly simple "My First Sony" line, Sony targeted its product directly to children. In doing so, they've created the next generation of loyal Sony buyers. Brilliant.

Today's weaned-on-television kids have been imprinted at an early impressionable age. They're the Latchkey kids who come home from school to an empty house and have to do the shopping: for detergents, dog foods, and frozen dinners. They're coupon-clippers and brand-name conscious. Think of the boy in *Home Alone* (smash movie), and how he bugged the checkout woman to find out if his choice of toothbrush was approved by the American Dental Association. Kids today know the right questions to ask.

On the serious side, it will be these same children who will force their parents to make environmentally and ethically correct buying decisions. Pity the mother who's still buying the family's fruit juices in dioxin-dyed cartons, or not recycling their aluminum cans.

If we go back to one of the most terrifying memories of the baby-boom generation, it was the nuclear drill at school. We were herded into the hallways and told to sit on the floor with our hands over our heads. To protect ourselves aginst nuclear attack! But think of the terror today. To have a child's imagination and hear about global warming, poisoned food, polluted water, bad air, and the burning of rainforests.

No wonder children are scared. The environment is the mushroom cloud of this generation. And the environment is the noble mission of the Children's Crusade. They recognize the health hazards they face are human-made. They understand they are in the process of becoming an endangered species. These are the next Vigilante Consumers.

And they will teach their parents.

Someday (soon) children will be able to communicate through their Nintendos to other children all over the planet. Kids will convince their peers to join the crusade to save the whales, save the water, save the world. In essence, to join forces in a cross-cultural crusade. And so its grows.

How do you reach the crusading children? Be like the sports-clothing company Patagonia, and annually give 10% of your profits to small-scale environmental causes, such as sponsoring schoolchildren to clean up a dying stream. Wear your Corporate Soul on your sleeve and tell them exactly who you are. Be honest. Their instincts are excellent. They cherish lived-up-to promises and real guarantees.

—Give the kids a special 800 number (for age 18 or younger).
—Make them your pen pals.
—Hire children to sit on your Board.
Then listen. And learn.

FUTURE SIGNALS

Out-of-the-frying-pan and into the future.

Trend Signals

What's next? What happens once everything on the shelves in all the stores is on-trend? When the diversity (and perversity) of human nature begins to reassert itself. Where will the next trends come from?

The best way to see early indications of "new" trends is to understand the evolution of our current trends. Trends go through different chartable stages. By the time a trend phases itself out, it will have gone through many transformations. For example, in the early eighties we observed that life was speeding up. We called it the Acceleration Syndrome. As that trend got faster, we re-named the trend 99 Lives. Women were holding down two jobs and raising a family. The fax machine increased our work week by spewing out a sheaf of ("get back to me tonight") papers, just as we were leaving the office. And mobile phones turned every place (cars, planes, taxis, trains) into mobile offices. 99 Lives accurately described a nation moving at breakneck speed. Toward nowhere.

In the same way, the trend Premium Quality gradually evolved to Quality (the word "premium" somehow suggested being overpriced). After the stock market crash of 1987, the Quality trend with its elitist overtones was narrowed down to Small Indulgences, reflecting a sudden sobriety. Forgoing the big-ticket items, people were consoling themselves with little treats—chocolates (4.5 billion lbs.), flowers, and expensive, ultrarich ice cream.

A future TrendFlash: Cocooning might change in the last part of 1992 into Burrowing, where consumers just can't take the heat, glaze over, and virtually disappear from the marketplace for a year or so.

Future future: Evolution will bring us out from under. We'll resurface from Burrowing and regroup into Clanning, a state-of-being where people will want to spend time with like people and form clans (from 20 to 20,000 members). Egonomics and niche marketing will gain new importance, as the need emerges for products targeted to Clanners.

One of the ways to sharpen your trend perception skills is to pay close attention to signals that flash in certain categories of news. At BrainReserve we carefully read any articles about:

- Food: new products, trendy restaurants, best-selling cookbooks.
- Any new product introductions, successful or not.
- Transformations in the family structure.
- Shifts in the workplace.
- The environment: are people motivated to change?
- The economy: is the fear level high?
- The overall cultural mood: anxious or hopeful?

If you use the current trends as a reference point, you'll be able to interpret things with an eye toward making trend connections on your own.

For example, you read: more neighborhoods are hiring armed

sentries. Make the *connection:* the Wandering Cocoon is deepening and we're witnessing the beginning of Burrowing.

You read: a new indoor "rock climbing" facility has opened up in your community. In Denver, Colorado, there are new store-sized indoor amusement parks called Big Fun which have bumper cars, mazes, a museum and café. *Connection:* Fantasy Adventure is taking consumers farther away from the real and the dangerous.

You see: apron-clad waitresses are now serving Whoppers to the table from 5 to 8 P.M. at 900 Burger Kings. *Connection:* Egonomics is entering the fast-food arena, taking away the hustle and hassle and offering personal attention and service.

You hear: someone has organized a major boycott against Evian water because they're still using unrefillable plastic bottles (this hasn't happened *yet!*). *Connection:* The Vigilante Consumer is getting angrier.

Or, you might notice that a trend is entering a new phase through new products in the making.

Let's say there's a new cigarette product (not here yet). It's only sold singly, made of the best tobacco, and elegantly wrapped like an afterdinner mint for special occasions. Sales take off. Possibly it's a new flip-side—or counter-trend to Staying Alive: maybe people are getting sick of being virtuous and think they can handle smoking just one. *Connection:* the success of such a product could be a sign of a New Decadence to watch for elsewhere. The Vigilante Consumer turns hedonistic.

The Gulf crisis focused us on the tragedy of oil-laden water. Even more than the *Valdez* did. We began to realize how important an ingredient water is to life sustenance, from sea-grass beds to dolphins to birds . . . to us. *Connection:* think, where does the water in soft drinks come from? Is there a national standard for water quality? (No, there's not.) *Connection:* the sodas we drink that are made in Maine may be purer than the ones we drink from New York. *Bigger connection:* the consumer wants to know not just the list of ingredients, but their origins. *Idea:* how come I care about the water I drink, but haven't given much thought about the water my baby drinks? *New product idea:* Baby Springs, pure water for babies from the Arctic Alaskan glacier springs.

And so these connections go.

But what if you've noticed something that seems entirely too obvious? Say, for example, you notice that at the onset of the Middle East war, all of your neighbors suddenly put out flagpoles and started raising the American flag every day.

The obvious: Patriotism is back.

The connection: America is hot.

The outcome: New confidence in American cars. American technology. A new belief in American blenders, bikes, and brands.

The signal is simple: The Patriot worked, didn't it? (Good name for a new car, a kid, or a dog.)

And if we can keep the quality up—and the pride—everything American-made will be the beneficiary.

An interview on a morning show with a Patriot factory worker, showing her care for the placement of every wire, brought a retro-flash to the '40s—Rosie the Riveter is back.

And that's how you read a signal, how you fly a trend. By looking up. From life.

Making It Big
(or Even Bigger)
in the '90s

"It's like déjà vu all over again."
attributed to YOGI BERRA

In business, a holding pattern is a retro-pattern. You can't just stay the same. The days when consumers were content to rely on the familiar are over. Tradition isn't enough. But sometimes the best *future* ideas are no further than your own background.

There are some brands, some famous names, that never die—or fade away. Some have been lying dormant and need Trend-Activating. Others, although giants, can even get bigger, better, sharper. For example:

—Green Giant: If they play their cards right, they would own the vegetarian direction (healthy, anti-cancer), and Sprout could start a new line for children.

—Bon Ami: Maybe the world has caught up with this safe, ecologically correct cleaner (so pure and nontoxic you can actually brush your teeth with it).

—Ford and Chrysler: If they bring back the '57 T-bird and the Town and Country station wagon with the guts of '90s technology, they could leverage the desire of Americans to buy American.

—Cream of Wheat: By restoring the old-fashioned imagery of this ultimate Mom/comfort food, they could create a retro-breakfast to compete with Quaker. It's the right thing to do.

—*Digestifs* (Fernet-Branca, grappa): After-dinner drinks of the '90s could capture a real health aura. Medicinal benefits—more fun than Alka-Seltzer.

—Speedy (as in Alka-Seltzer): Bring back the name! For instant repair kiosks for TV's, faxes, car phones, answering machines. What a relief it would be to harried, high-tech consumers!

—Schwinn: A new age of New Age bikers will want to experience the Rolls-Royce of bicycles.

—Haig & Haig Pinch: As we drink less but better, we'll want to drink more of this fabled Scotch. The pinched bottle brings back the glamour drinking of the early fifties.

—Timex: As our concerns expand from "getting there on time" to "staying home safe," there's a big opportunity for Timex to provide affordable, install-it-yourself security systems.

—Tupperware: Out of the kitchen and into the garden! How about a line of gardening tools (or just plain tools) sold at home, with a lifetime Tupperware guarantee.

—Levi's: Americans love to live in Levi's. The time is right for a national chain of rough, tough dude-ranch hotels.

—Merck: Building on their trusted name in medicine, Merck could create and open the coming industry of "foodaceuticals"— offering "healthful eating plans" with mind/body foods sold by mail order.

—Kleenex: Hypoallergenic cleaning products, to eliminate dust, pollen, and toxins, are a natural jump into the future for this "antisneeze" company.

—Miles One-a-Day Vitamins: This company heads into the millennium and beyond with a patch that releases vitamins and minerals into your bloodstream as your body needs them.

—Pathfinder: Their future lies in their name. They could forge new paths by expanding into travel books, audio or video tapes, atlases, maps, and flashlights.

—McDonald's: From "feeding children" to "feeding and entertaining" children to . . . the future for McDonald's could be in a chain of child-care centers, an ethical (and profitable) position to be in for the coming years.

—Jeep: Why not a hit-the-road, adventure-style line of camping gear and clothing (for campers and camper wannabe's)?

—Apple Computer: With its high-tech "make-it-easy," "do-it-fun" corporate ethos, Apple is perfectly positioned to introduce a line of learning disability centers, to offer computer-eased help for dyslexics and stutterers.

—Carter's: They once owned "bedtime." Carter's could own bedtime even more in a New Age with a lulling, herbal-sleep drink for children.

—Whitman's: The American traditional chocolatier (each candy identified) could answer the needs of Down-Agers, Staying Alivers, and 99 Livers with a Fresh Dessert Sampler for both drug and convenience stores.

—Buster Brown: A company that could again revolutionize the shoe industry with custom-fitting of children's shoes—through sonograms. (Remember X-ray fittings from your childhood?) This would be safe nostalgia cum customization.

—Perdue: The king of chicken could bring his Hot-Branding concept to fish farming, the growth food area of the future.

—Johnson & Johnson: The people who care so well for babies should open a chain of (work-related) communities for the elderly. A whole-life-caring corporation!

Now it's your turn to think of more.

FlashForward '90s

If you know the future, it's pretty easy to figure out the present.   1990

The news is good. We'll finally learn how to maximize our technology—stretch our resources and save our souls.

The tonality of this decade will be consumers' inner resources opposing external dangers and threats: economic, criminal, ethical, environmental.

Nonviolence will be a theme—from therapy to food. The primal screaming sessions of a decade or two ago (doesn't primal screaming sound redundant now?) will turn passively serene, into tomorrow's new brain clinics where doses of light invigorate and relax you at the same time.

We'll want nonviolent food, too. It might be debatable whether vegetables cry when plucked from the vine, but it's clear that we don't want food that gets treated cruelly in order to get on our plate. Think back to k. d. lang's "Meat Stinks" campaign against the brutal slaughtering of beef. And the press for bigger, better chicken coops. Fashion, too, has heard this same message: No more fur from wild creatures, no more leg traps.

The strengthening of inner resources will turn into a big business—Mood Food; Self-care; Stress Management; and Environmental Appliances, such as poison-sensitive rods to filter and test the air, water, and food.

Futureforward

These are some new thoughts, some new business ideas which I predict might take us plunging into the near, and the far, future.

Controlled Escape: Computers will take us on mind-trips to Africa, the Brazilian rainforest, the Himalayas. Or time-travel us back to the French Revolution or to our own safe childhoods or those of our parents and grandparents.

The Age of the Brain: The late '90s will bring a new respect for "thinking to survive." We learned that pure technology and brute force didn't get us very far. A quest for knowledge will take over and be strengthened in places like Brain Gyms, where we will exercise our thinking, and Brain Clubs, where we will play mind games (an enormous new industry that started in the '80s with Nintendo). Great for those kids who've become "brain-lax" because of an over-reliance on calculators and computers. We'll be able to buy thinking-herbs and creativity-waters that sharpen our wits, increase our powers.

Time Out: In an environment that's drying up ecologically, ethically, and educationally, the ultimate luxury vacation will be a year off from the grind. This one-year-out-of-mainstream sabbatical becomes the Indulgence of the '90s, creating a new industry of "noncareer" advisers, planners, and destinations.

Beauty-as-Science: Time-release, face-lift implants will de-age you ever so gradually. Reconstructive surgery, to make you taller, bigger, stronger, straighter, with better sight and hearing.

Eco-Settling: Giving it all up to go to a cleaner, healthier, safer place. For good. And for the good of your children.

Expanded Family: People (married or not, alone or together) adopting infants, children, and other adults less fortunate than they are.

Children as Experts: We finally recognize the power, insight, and intuition of children and turn to them for expert advice, placing them on our most important boards, electing them to political office, and making them peace arbitrators. "And a little child shall lead us" is the late '90s anti-war cry.

Own Your Own Android: You won't see humans driving buses, at supermarket check outs, or serving up fast (slow) food. They'll be replaced by colonies of androids who can walk your dog or fight your war. They don't belong to unions either.

Composting Industry: Easy, do-it-yourself compost bins (air-tight) will be in the kitchen, and enclosed heaps in every backyard. Reducing-your-own-garbage becomes big business with compost consultants, books, videos, and equipment.

Security-Screen: A hand-held, remote control unit will guard your front door, watch over your baby, scan the grounds, give you messages, and even turn off the pot roast.

Dream Architects: A new consulting business will help individuals identify and implement their dream life. We'll learn how to make our "dreams come true" over short, medium, or long periods of time, in business, the arts, sciences.

Baby Stops: To lighten up the stroller. Fast-food places will offer fast but healthy baby food—in department stores, amusement parks, or on the road.

The New Heroes: Ecological saviors—from those scientists that clean up oil spills to a pop-series character called Eco-Man. Watch for the new "hot" master's degree, an M.A. in Ecology.

Emerging Medicine/Law Clinics: Not staffed with full-fledged M.D.'s or lawyers, but associates who know the system well enough to give first aid/fast help—from injections and prescriptions, to advice.

Good-Guy Scanner: A small portable computer that will tell you the sociological, ecological, ethical stance of any company in the supermarket. It will check weights by laser, even tally your total.

Lost and Found Chip: A micro-chip that a dentist implants in a child's tooth or under the skin will track him through life via satellite anywhere in the world.

This Is the
First Chapter
of My Next Book

Because you can't stop looking at the future.

Trends never end.

(And the future is never here.)

So, once you've read this, you'll have to say: "Next, next, and next."

Glossary

BRAINRESERVE TRENDS

Cashing Out: Working women and men, questioning personal/ career satisfaction and goals, opt for simpler living.

Cocooning: The need to protect oneself from the harsh, unpredictable realities of the outside world.

Down-Aging: Nostalgic for their carefree childhood, baby boomers find comfort in familiar pursuits and products of their youth.

Egonomics: The sterile computer era breeds the desire to make a personal statement.

Fantasy Adventure: Modern age whets our desire for roads untaken.

99 Lives: Too fast a pace, too little time, causes societal schizophrenia and forces us to assume multiple roles and adapt easily.

S.O.S. (Save Our Society): The country rediscovers a social conscience of ethics, passion, and compassion.

Small Indulgences: Stressed-out consumers want to indulge in affordable luxuries and seek ways to reward themselves.

Staying Alive: Awareness that good health extends longevity leads to a new way of life.

The Vigilante Consumer: The consumer manipulates marketers and the marketplace through pressure, protest, and politics.

BRAINRESERVE TERMS

Acceleration Syndrome, The: The speeding up of everyone's lives to a breakneck pace.

Adrenaline Adjusting: Transferring the energy that comes from the expectation of disaster into positive action. A source of strength to change the future.

AdverNews: A future customized newspaper, printed off your home computer screen; made up of advertisements, coupons, news.

Armored Cocoon: A second-decade evolution of the trend Cocooning, in which paranoia industries and security systems "arm the fortress."

Boomerang Kids: Adult children who leave the nest, find the world too harsh, and return to live at home.

Brailling the Culture: Monitoring cultural signals—magazines, newspapers, books, videos, movies, TV, music, events, food fads—in order to "feel out" future trends.

BrainJam: BrainReserve ideation sessions that use the trends as a springboard for generating ideas. A proprietary "ThinkTank."

BrainReserve: A marketing consultancy; a small, caring clinic for future thinking. Founded in 1974.

Brand Renewal: A BrainReserve service to breathe new life into fading brands.

Burrowing: The ultimate expression of Cocooning in which consumers dig in, ever deeper, with a bunker mentality.

Children's Crusade: A coming social and cultural phenomenon in which children are the driving force to save the planet.

Clanning: The grouping together of people on the basis of some commonality: blood relationships, special interests, political causes, shared tastes, in a "social cocoon."

Concern for Wellness: Desire for good health (and fitness); fear of illness and rising medical costs.

ConsumerSpeak: A language, used by consumers, that does not always mean what they say. You need to ConsumerListen to come up with the truth.

ConsumerTime: A timeline, tied to the trends, to tell you precisely when a product is ready to market.

Corporate Soul: A decency positioning for any company that wants to establish a close relationship with its consumer, based on trust. It means full public disclosure of its political and environmental stances.

Counter-Trends: The flip-side of a trend. Doing something totally opposite. A good example is Fitness/Fatness (exercising: Staying Alive; then eating sweets: Small Indulgences).

Couture for the Masses: Making quality, customized, individually created products, available on a large-scale basis.

Creative Think: A step in BrainReserve's proprietary methodology. An ideation session, held with carefully screened TalentBank members or highly articulate consumers, to generate a brainstorm of ideas.

Critical Think: A step in BrainReserve's proprietary methodology in which BrainReserve staff evaluates the results of BrainJams and Creative Thinks, by screening them through the trends.

Decency Decade, The: The decade of the '90s in which companies and consumers will revert to traditional values. A commitment to the three E's: Environment, Education, Ethics.

Decency Positioning, The: A corporate policy to "be good, do good"; to create a relationship with the consumer that's based on trust.

Decession: Recessionary spending against a backdrop of depressionary thinking.

Discontinuity Trend Analysis: A methodology in which ideas, products, businesses, and other targets are analyzed against the trends as a way of evaluating their potential for the future.

DOBY's: Acronym for Daddy Older, Baby Younger. A new life-stage group of older fathers, often on their second (or third) reproductive round. (*See also* MOBY's).

Extremism: Projecting a business or concept to its darkest future scenario, then bringing it back, via the trends, to set a present course of action.

Fanzines: Periodic publications with highly specialized readership targets.

Fight Back: The Conscious Consumer struggles to exert influence over the environment, government, and products.

Flex-time: The flexible structuring of work hours to accommodate employees' family responsibilities, and special needs.

Flip-sides: The other side of the story, as it applies to trends. (*See also* Counter-Trends.)

Folking of America, The: A cultural phenomenon in which plain, simple "country" values and philosophers acquire high mainstream appeal.

Foodaceuticals: A new food industry of the future. Food, beyond simple nourishment—with medicinal qualities, consumed for health reasons.

FutureFocus: A BrainReserve product that provides marketing strategies and concepts with sharp long-term competitive advantages.

FutureForward: New business ideas for the year, and far future.

Global Kids: A new generation of children who see themselves as citizens of the world. Marked by a strong concern for the future.

Hoffices (Home/Offices): The building, furnishing, equipping, and "servicing" of home offices, a big business opportunity for the future.

HomeComing: Professional women question corporate life and opt for new ventures, adventures, (even) motherhood.

Home Reality Engine: The home computer that runs the software that creates Virtual Reality. (*See also* Virtual Reality.)

Hot-Branding: Products or companies that stand above the crowd, by virtue of character, style, quality, and personality.

Huddling and Cuddling: A particular form of the Socialized Cocoon in which people come together for shared comfort and a sense of safety.

Indulging at Discount: A market phenomenon in which people are looking for high-ticket, prestige products at rock-bottom prices.

InfoBuying: A future home computer scanning system. The Consumer asks InfoBank for shopping information, then, computer-orders (or InfoBuys) the selections.

Latch-Key Kids: A population segment made up of children who come home from school to an empty home. They "let themselves in"; are responsible for food shopping and cooking.

Log Cabin Chic: A style based on an affection for the homespun, the primitive, the look and feel of the American Frontier. Especially, home furnishings and clothing.

MOBY's: Acronym for Mommy Older, Baby Younger. A new population segment of women having babies later in life. (*See also* DOBY's.)

Mood Food: A form of "foodaceuticals." Food that you consume for specific emotional benefits: to calm down, be energized, combat depression, gain a "competitive edge."

New Age Arrogance: A cultural phenomenon brought about by aging baby boomers in which "over 40" is given more prestige than "under 30."

New Decadence: A possible new T.I.P. (Trend-in-Progress).

New Health Age Adults: Consumers who consider their health and the health of the planet top priorities.

1000#: One step beyond the 800# and 900#, it will be a more expensive consumer-pay call, 24 hours, 7 days a week, for real help, real information.

Preventive Business: A method of using the trends to reprioritize or diversify an off-trend company. Taking action before disaster strikes.

PUPPYs: Acronym for Poor Urban Professionals.

Retro-Aging: The youthful mind-set for the '90s.

Sandwichers: A new life-stage group. Adults caught in middle life with long-term dual responsibilities: caring for their children and their aging parents.

Saloning and Salooning: An aspect of the Socialized Cocoon, in which casually organized small groups gather in homes to pursue common interests, or venture out as social cocoons to local bars and restaurants.

ScreenMail: A future home computer process of shopping, paying bills, getting/sending information.

Second Opinion: A BrainReserve service that evaluates a company's plans (sales, marketing or new products) in light of the trends.

SKIPPIE's: An acronym for School Kids with Incomes and Purchasing Power. A growing and powerful population segment.

Socialized Cocoon: Inviting select friends into your cocoon to share comfort and combat loneliness. (*See also* "Huddling and Cuddling.")

Socioquake: The coming, total transformation of mainstream America.

Streamlining: A response to the 99 Lives trend, in which consumers pare down and edit their lives.

Survivor Kids: Children of a new generation whose major preoccupation is survival: either their own (at the lower end of the socio-economic scale), or that of the planet. (*See also* Global Kids.)

TalentBank: BrainReserve's computerized network of more than 2,000 smart people to call on; the company's brainy-idea reserve.

Three "E's": The big concerns for the future of America: Environment, Education, and Ethics.

Time Elasticity: The phenomenon of ConsumerTime slowing down, speeding up, or briefly stopping, in response to outside events, or to the trends themselves.

T.I.P.: A BrainReserve Trend-in-Progress; a possibly emerging trend from signals in the marketplace.

TrendAction: A BrainReserve product that combines TrendView with a BrainJam; to generate 75–200 unique, trend-driven ideas.

TrendBank: The repository of BrainReserve's trend information, a database made up of culture monitoring and consumer interviews.

TrendBending: The process of "reshaping" a product, business, or idea to the trends, to move them closer to consumer wants and needs. A corrrection or modification to ensure longevity.

TrendFlash: Hot news!

TrendPack: A bimonthly subscription service through which BrainReserve clients receive 3-dimensional samples of the trends, as well as pointers on how to apply them to their businesses.

TrendsLens: A way of viewing the world through the focused lens of the trends.

TrendTalk: A language with only a future tense.

TrendTime: The life span of a trend, usually at least ten years.

TrendTracking: A method of following the evolutions of a trend along a timeline. Or, the act of looking for evidence of existing or emerging trends. A function of the BrainReserve TrendBank.

TrendTrek: A market check or "field trip" to a cutting-edge location that stimulates fresh thinking about new products and services.

TrendView: A seminar presentation of BrainReserve's overview of the future: its trends and trend-identifying process; questions and answers.

TrendVision: A trend-based ability to open up your eyes and see the future coming.

Trophy Kids: Overindulged children, born of older parents who view these young ones as another career achievement.

Truth in Advertising: New wave of consumer-oriented advertising where all product claims are verified and objectively presented truths are told.

Twisting the Familiar: Turning something comfortable into something new. Designing a new product with familiar benefits.

Universal Screen Test: A filter to organize what one sees, hears, and reads in order to test where the market is headed.

Virtual Reality: A technology that makes it possible to synthesize a seemingly real, interactive world through computer-generated images and sensations.

Wandering Cocoon: Bringing the comfort and coziness of the home cocoon to means of transportation: the car, mini-van, train, airplane.

WOOFs: Acronym for Well-Off Older Folks. A growing population with special consumer wants and needs and significant purchasing power.

BrainReserve
Reading List

This is a selection of what we read (usually three people, three hours a day) and incorporate into our TrendBank. To look for support of trends and contradictions/flip-sides and sidelights.

General Interest/Information
Time
Newsweek
People
New York
Modern Maturity
Essence
Emerge
California Magazine
Vanidades
Women
Vogue
Elle
Sassy
Mirabella
Lear's
Good Housekeeping
Working Mother
New York Woman
Harper's Bazaar
Mademoiselle
Victoria
Ladies' Home Journal
Allure
W
BBW (Big Beautiful Women)

READING LIST

Men
Esquire
Gentlemen's Quarterly
Men's Health
M, inc.
Details

News
The New York Times
The Wall Street Journal
USA Today
The Washington Post
Newsday
U.S. News & World Report
Le Monde

Science
Discover
Technology Review
The Futurist
Omni
Science Digest

Health
American Health
Longevity
Self
In Health
Health Watch
Vegetarian Journal
Changes

Food/Liquor
Bon Appétit
Gourmet
Food & Wine
Eating Well
Vegetarian Times

Home
Metropolitan Home
HG
Architectural Digest

Travel/International
Conde Nast Traveler
European Travel & Life
Travel & Leisure
Soviet Life
Tokyo Journal
Harper's & Queen
Marie Claire
Arena
Elegance (Netherlands)

Entertainment/Gossip
Interview
National Enquirer
L.A. Style
Vanity Fair
Entertainment Weekly
Premiere
TV Guide
Billboard
Variety
Rolling Stone

Literary/Art
The New Yorker
Granta
The Quarterly: New American
    Writing
Journal of Popular Culture
Publishers Weekly
The Atlantic
Harper's
Art & Antiques
Grand Street

Business
Fortune
Forbes
Business Week
Entrepreneur
Inc.
Business Ethics

Economics
The Economist
Japan Economic Journal

Politics
The Nation
New Republic
The Manchester Guardian

The Washington Spectator
Politique Internationale
Reason
Z
Mother Jones

Environment
Garbage
Greenpeace
Earthwatch
Buzzworm
E: The Environmental Magazine
The Earthwise Consumer
The Amicus Journal
EcoSource

Newsletters and Trade Publications
John Naisbitt's Trend Letter
Mayo Clinic Health Letter
Tufts Nutrition Letter
Berkeley Wellness Letter
Research Alert
Consumer Confidence Survey
The Art of Eating
Britchkey Restaurant Letter
New Product News
Food Industry Newsletter
Food Marketing Briefs

Food & Beverage Marketing
Market Watch: The Wines, Spirits, & Beer Business
Top Shelf: Barkeeping At Its Best
Chain Drug Review
National Home Center News
Supermarket News
Consumer Reports
National Boycott News
Advertising Age
Adweek's Marketing Week

New Age
New Age
Whole Earth Review
East West
Yoga Journal
Design Spirit
New Realities

Offbeat
Utne Reader
Libido: The Journal of Sex and Sensibility
Monk: Public Diary of the Pilgrim's Journey
Paper
Outweek

Appendix: How the Future Looks to the Fortune 500 (and Others)

Soothing Thoughts.

"We'll soon see a dramatic development in "enabling drugs"—i.e., anti-stress drugs. Although we know about the future of semi-conductors, we still haven't figured out how to control the biochemistry of the brain. But control it we will."

—Ian A. Martin, Chairman & CEO
Grand Metropolitan Food Sector

The Barometer of Initiative.

"People talk about market fluctuations. My feeling is that markets climb up or down, based on the initiative and creativity of the people who make up the marketplace. Our market goes up when we're initiating, inventing, and creating. And down when we're stagnant or at a standstill."

—Robert M. Phillips, Chairman & CEO
Unilever Personal Products Group USA

Next on Line.
"Traditional trademarks and brands will exist in the future as they do today. But through computer technology and modems or voice mail, you'll be able to call one central location for all your household needs for the next thirty days—and you'll pick up your order at that place, like picking up dry-cleaning."

—Michael K. Lorelli, President
Pepsi-Cola East

Be Good, Do Good.
"Using feminine principles in business is wonderful—leading a company with gut feelings, instinct, intuition, passion. Very strong female ethics revolve around the concept of caring and sharing, and I still believe that women can change the marketplace."

—Anita Roddick, Managing Director
The Body Shop International PLC

Marketing Inside and Out.
"More and more service companies are awakening to the fact that their internal employee constituency is one of their most important target markets. The better employees feel about themselves and their company—the better they feel about the customer."

—Michael W. Gunn
Senior Vice President
Marketing
American Airlines

Optics on the Future.
"Fiber optics will change the makeup of cities. Employees will be able to serve their companies from miles away, thus reducing the requirement for large urban office masses."

> —Henry E. Kates
> President & CEO
> Mutual Benefit Life

Principles That Never Die.
"Trends will come and trends will go, but meeting the needs of your customer, taking care of your employees, and being responsible to the communities in which we live and work are basic values that will never go out of style. They will also lead to long-term gains for any corporation's stockholders. These principles, embodied in the one-hundred-year-old Johnson & Johnson credo, will still be in style in one hundred years.

> —Brian D. Perkins
> Director of Product Management
> McNeil Consumer Products Company

The Might of Right.
"No matter what changes occur in distribution and retailing, it will always be a brand game. Businesses will continue to be built on successful brands with the right values. In foods and beverages, great taste is, of course, the first essential, but the great brands of tomorrow will also need to have the right nutritional properties."

> —William G. Pietersen
> President
> Seagram Beverage Group

There are the Builders and the conservators.
"America became great with the builders, but where are they today? All we have are guardians. Let's get on with it and build again!"

> —Leonard A. Lauder
> President & CEO
> Estée Lauder Companies

Watch for New Mail.

"As postal rates climb at a rate far greater than inflation, the United States Postal Service is definitely going to face serious competition. There are an increasing number of alternatives available to traditional big-volume mailers."

—Reginald K. Brack, Jr.
Chairman, President & CEO
Time Warner Publishing

A Chicken in Every Greenhouse.

"In the future we're going to see greenhouses incorporated into apartments and houses, and people will be growing their own vegetables and herbs, maybe even chickens and pigs. The greenhouse will be as important in a home as the bathroom."

—Michel Roux, President
Carillon Importers, Ltd.

Faster Than a Speeding Bullet.

"What worries me is that the 'cycle time' regulating the ups and downs of business is getting shorter, and that some of the peaks and valleys are getting higher and lower. You have to be on your toes a lot more than in the past. You have to be able not to panic or overact. Sureness and steadiness worked for my dad's generation. But now, it's reaction time."

—I. M. Booth, President & CEO
Polaroid Corporation

The Challenge of Diversity.

"There'll be more diversity among our consumers, our customers and our business colleagues. To recognize, value and effectively address this growing diversity in the marketplace and workplace will be the exciting business challenge of the '90s."

—Ellen Marram, President & CEO
Nabisco Biscuit Company

The New Leader.
"The business leadership of the future will not resemble that of the past. Leadership's role will be to create the 'vision' for the company and to cultivate a culture that listens—listens to its customers, listens to its employees, and then empowers them. The old command-and-control style of leadership will not work in a complex environment that changes rapdily, communicates instantly, and relies on a diverse workforce for results. Future leadership will need to set high goals, define the standards, create the culture, and let the organization do the rest."

> —Martin J. Pazzani
> Vice President, Marketing
> Heublein, Inc.

A-B-C, Uno, Dos, Tres.
"There's no simple answer to our many problems, but there's one fundamental: The public school system is at the root of a democratic society. And a culture that's not literate, particularly today, is a culture at great risk. Fixing the school system is our most important problem."

> —John R. Opel
> Chairman of the Executive Committee
> International Business Machines Corporation

The End of Small Talk.
"Personal relationships are going to become more strained because more people will depend on computers to do business. There'll be even less interaction and people-skills won't be as well-honed as they are now. The art of reading and conversation are going to be lost. It's happening to our young people now. No small talk. That's a real threat to the integrity of a culture."

> —Ellen Merlo
> Vice President, Marketing Services
> Philip Morris U.S.A.

Stores Without Walls.
"I think we'll see a major extension of mail order, to where we punch up mysterious machines to order groceries and everything else we need.

We'll go to stores, not because we have to, but because we want to, for the socialization of it."

—Ronald Ahrens
Consumer Group President
Bristol-Myers Squibb

A New Fusion of Business and Politics.
"Eventually, more business people will get involved in making the political process work again. Hopefully, in the future, it will be safe to run for office. The media will stop destroying reputations, and focus instead on what a person's contribution could be."

—Richard Gillman
Chairman of the Board
Bally's Park Place Casino Hotel

The Refuge of History.
"I don't find all this 'looking back' to the past surprising. It's just part of a well-regulated society—you're always trying to define where you're going by where you've been. In a future-minded society like ours, it's a means of projecting the old days onto the new, so we can somehow fuse the two and create a controlled and familiar universe. History, even if it's 1950s history, is safe."

—C. Duncan Rice, Dean
Faculty of Arts & Science
New York University

The Corporate Educator.
"I don't think it is inherently up to the corporation to educate, but any corporation today which is cognizant of the alternative will inevitably take on that responsibility. In the absence of anything else, corporations will pick up the education reins."

—Phillip J. Riese
Executive Vice President
& General Manager
Personal Card Division
American Express Company

The Future Is Down the Road.

"We're working on biodegradable bottles. It's not a program that is imminent, because there are significant behavioral changes the consumers will first have to accept. It's a question of whether you think the future is five or ten or twenty years down the road. We'll see better, more flexible, more structurally sound plastics and other kinds of packaging and/or chemical innovations that just aren't apparent now."

—Brian McFarland, President
Personal Care Division
The Gillette Company

Born-Again Business.

"Business will be reborn. It'll break out and people will begin to start little businesses that in turn will compete with the conglomerates, then *become* the new conglomerates. That'll be the cycle."

—Herbert M. Baum, President
Campbell North America
Campbell Soup Company

On Borrowed Time.

"How can you be the world's leading power when you're the world's leading borrower? It's the lenders who have the leverage."

—Peter G. Peterson, Chairman
The Blackstone Group

Where Is Harry?

"There's a happening going on that I call the 'loss of accumulated wisdom.' American companies are very busy now weeding out those older employees with twenty or thirty years of service. But what happens when they stop rearranging personnel and go back to running the business? The dialogue will go something like: 'Well, how did we do this?' 'I don't know; Harry always used to handle it when he was inventory control manager.' 'So, where the hell is Harry?' 'He's one we let go on the early retirement program.' Those things catch up and affect the character of a particular business. The wisdom being lost now is eventually going to hurt our corporations."

—Peter N. Rogers, President & CEO
E. J. Brach Corp.

The Precious Cost of Working.
"Women are realizing now that it's hard to be Super Woman. It isn't so great to double your family's income, if it means you have to turn your back on your family and your home."

—Martha Stewart
Martha Stewart, Inc.

Shopping as Distraction.
"The thrill of going through a large, multiproduct discount store, department store, or mall will increasingly take on more and more entertainment flavor. It won't be the hands-on experience of simply buying what you need."

—Peter M. Palermo, Vice President
& General Manager
Consumer Imaging Division
Eastman Kodak Company

Do the Right Thing.
"Are corporate ethics an oxymoron? What exactly is the role of the corporation today? In a very real way, we're in a marvelous transition period. In the fifties, you had Auden and *The Age of Anxiety*, Eliot and *The Hollow Men* and the Existentialists. Now we're fighting that sense of helplessness. There's a new moral appeal in the air. Maybe we don't know how to do it yet, but we want to buy the right product with the right packaging from the right company."

—Sam Keen, Author

Prosperity in the Infrastructure.
"Tangible prosperity is visible all throughout Europe, even where the economy itself is weak. People are, in fact, in many ways living to

a higher standard of life than we are. Even in England, which has seen its share of bad times, prosperity is manifest. The English have spent a lot of money on roads that are smooth, sidewalks that are swept, parks that are clean, neat and well-maintained. We, on the other hand, have ignored the infrastructure, which is where *quality* of life is."

—Sandra Myer
Senior Officer, Corporate Affairs
Citibank, N.A.

Let Us See Your Face.
"Anonymous marketing just doesn't work anymore. Consumers want to know not only *what* they're buying, but *who* they're buying it from. The *people*, not the *logo*. Consumer relationship development is as important as product development."

—Frank P. Perdue
Chairman of the Board
Perdue Farms Inc.

Insecure at the Office.
"The biggest thing that has happened in the last decade is that no one now feels secure. You can't cut forty percent of a company and have the sixty percent remaining assume that they have a job for life. I think the Japanese will be feeling it next. Once that over-extended economy starts letting people off, the whole concept of what Japan stands for—lifetime employment, loyalty to company—will be shattered."

—Jay Chiat, Chairman/CEO Worldwide
Chiat/Day/Mojo/ Inc. Advertising

High Cost of Cheating.
"Companies are realizing that not being ethical can be very expensive. We're seeing lawsuits in record numbers . . . record settlements where corporations have cut corners."

—Mary Cunningham Agee
Executive Director
The Nurturing Network

Nostalgia About Yesterday.
"Nostalgia, that deep wistfulness for the past, is affecting people at a much younger age now than it ever did before. It used to be that only people who had reached a certain level of maturity looked back at the good ol' days. Now people in their late thirties, early forties, are becoming increasingly nostalgic about the recent past. Other generations used to focus more on the questions of the future."

—Adam Hanft, President
& Creative Director
Slater Hanft Martin, Inc.

Small Indulgences Can Be Big Business.
"Twelve or fifteen years ago, when I started going to Europe frequently, I came across those beautifully lacquered Dupont pens. Back then, a good business pen sold for twelve or fifteen dollars—and these were the equivalent of one hundred and twenty-five dollars. For the first time, it registered with me how far people would stretch for something special. For just one hundred dollars you could have something absolutely excellent—what I call an 'affordable perk.' That desire will escalate even more in the future."

—Leslie H. Wexner
Chairman of the Board & CEO
The Limited, Inc.

Proud Cynics.
"After five years in the States, I've changed my mind about prospects for the future. The tremendous asset in this country is the people. Americans, by and large, have a positive attitude about the future which is very different from Europeans, who are much more cynical because of their history. And they're proud of being cynical."

—Patrick Choel
Chairman
Elida Gibbs-Fabergé
Paris, France

Friendly Persuasions.
"The magic new ingredient has always been inside the *product*. Now it will be outside, in the packaging. And 'environmentally friendly' prod-

210

ucts will be more important than 'natural,' the buzz-label of the last decade. There'll also be a renaissance in the aroma business—air fresheners in new forms, lotions with fragrance that will help you relax or go to sleep."

—Cornelius J. Goeren, Director
New Product Development
The Mennen Company

Strength in Inventiveness.

"Big ideas" are going to push America ahead in business and help us to outdistance the competition from abroad. Corporations and individuals will need to agree on priorities for our society and then make them happen. There may indeed be an international economy on the verge of burgeoning, and Americans will need to compete for our fair share of the international dollar. Our inventiveness and foresightedness are going to be called on as never before."

—Sander A. Flaum
President/CEO
Robert A. Becker, Inc.

Rekindle the Spirit.

"It's not that Americans are getting lazier, it's that we're more disheartened. There isn't a feeling anymore of extraordinary opportunity—a sense that anything is possible. When I started out, I thought that we, as a country, could conquer all odds, bridge any frontier. I don't think my children feel that way. We need to recapture that spirit."

—Carole Isenberg, Big Light Films

Shifting Down, Cashing Out.

"The corporate world is a stagnant, superficial, unsatisfying, dishonest, horrible environment. Why would anybody want to join it? The smart person is sitting back and reevaluating all the options, saying I don't need this, and leaving. We'll be seeing a shift from manufacturing-driven businesses to service-oriented businesses. Entrepreneurs: Your time is now."

—Marquis Visich de Visoko
Knight-Grand Cross

Future Faith.

"The only thing about the future of which I'm certain is that I am going to live forever."

—Arthur T. Shorin, CEO
The Topps Company, Inc.

The More Things Change.

"I don't think the world changes very much. There's no reason to believe that the ethical environment today is any better or worse than it was thirty, fifty or a hundred years ago. It ebbs, it flows. The good news now is that for everybody who is losing his or her soul to a corporation, there are ten others who are starting a business or who are working in an environment where they own a piece of it. *The Organization Man* was written a long time ago. *Death of a Salesman* was written a long time ago. I don't know that corporate America is any more hostile than it ever was."

—Dick West, Dean
Leonard N. Stern School of Business
New York University

Natural Law Is the Prevailing Law.

"We all have to abide by it or we'll perish. The road to the future is very short. The human being has challenged time. He says: Look at my technology. I have a chain saw and can cut down that black walnut tree in fifteen minutes. It'll take a hundred and fifty years to grow that tree again.

The environment will continue as the issue of the nineties. It's going to be the cause of population displacement, disease, questionable food—it's all interrelated. We won't have wars about Communism and capitalism—they'll be about land and natural resources."

—Chief Oren Lyons, Iroquois tribes

BRAINRESERVE METHODOLOGY FLOW CHART

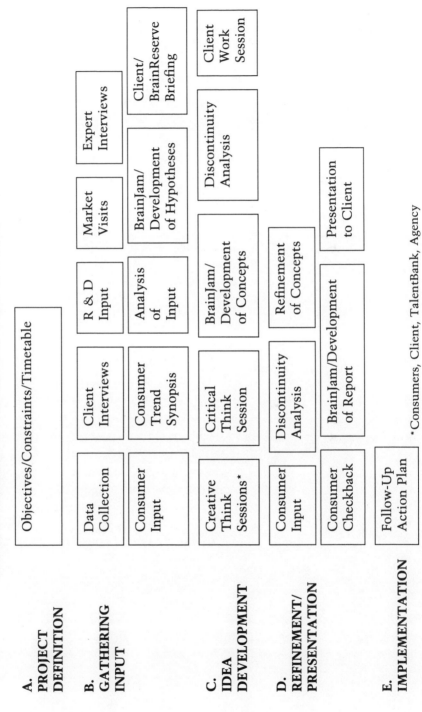

A.
PROJECT
DEFINITION

Objectives/Constraints/Timetable

B.
GATHERING
INPUT

| Data Collection | Client Interviews | R & D Input | Market Visits | Expert Interviews |
| Consumer Input | Consumer Trend Synopsis | Analysis of Input | BrainJam/ Development of Hypotheses | Client/ BrainReserve Briefing |

C.
IDEA
DEVELOPMENT

| Creative Think Sessions* | Critical Think Session | BrainJam/ Development of Concepts | Discontinuity Analysis | Client Work Session |

D.
REFINEMENT/
PRESENTATION

| Consumer Input | Discontinuity Analysis | Refinement of Concepts |
| Consumer Checkback | BrainJam/Development of Report | Presentation to Client |

E.
IMPLEMENTATION

Follow-Up Action Plan

*Consumers, Client, TalentBank, Agency

BrainReserve
Client List

"Thank you to all the clients who helped build BrainReserve."

*American Express Inc.
 Financial Services

*American Telephone & Telegraph
 Telecommunications

*Anheuser-Busch, Inc.
 Beer Products

Avon Products, Inc.
 Cosmetics

*Bacardi Imports, Inc.
 Distilled Spirits

Bally's Park Place Casino Hotel
Travel & Leisure

*Beatrice/Hunt-Wesson
Food Products

The Black & Decker Corporation
Home Appliances

*Borden, Inc.
Beverages

*Bristol-Myers Company
Vitamins
Cough/Cold Products

*Campbell Soup Company
Food Products

*Carillon Importers Ltd.
Distilled Spirits

*Chesebrough-Pond's Inc.
Deodorants
Bar Soaps
Shampoos
Skin-Care Products

*Citibank, N.A.
Financial Services

*The Clorox Company
Food Products
Health & Beauty Aids
Household Products

Coca-Cola USA
Soft drinks

*Colgate-Palmolive Company
Oral Hygiene Products
Skin Care Products
Hair Care Products
Dishwashing Liquids

*Continental Baking Company
Bread Products
Cake Products

*Eastman Kodak Company
The Future of Photography

Estée Lauder
Men's Cologne
and Related Products

Fisher-Price
Toys & Juvenile Products

*General Foods Corporation
Coffee, Food Products

*The Gillette Company (Paper Mate Division)
Stationary Products
Shampoos

The Hearst Corporation
Publishing

*Hoffmann-La Roche, Inc.
Pharmaceuticals

*International Business Machines Corp.
Personal Computers

*Johnson & Johnson Products, Inc.
Analgesics

*Kimberly-Clark Corporation
Health and Beauty Aids
Home Health-Care Products
Industrial/Institutional Products

Kobrand Corporation
Distilled Spirits

Lever Brothers Company
Household Products
Health and Beauty Aids
Fragrances

MasterCard International
Financial Services

MCI Telecommunications Corporation
Telecommunications

*McNeil Consumer Products Company
Analgesics

Mutual Benefit Life
Life Insurance

*Nabisco Brands USA
Food Products

Nestlé Foods Corporation
Diet Food Products

New York Life Insurance Company
Life Insurance

*Nissan Research and Development
Automobiles

People Magazine
Publishing

*Pepsi-Cola Company
Soft-Drink Products

*Pfizer Inc.
Hair-Care Products
Fragrances

*Philip Morris International
Nontobacco Products

*The Pillsbury Company
Food Products
Restaurants

*Polaroid Corporation
Photography

*The Procter & Gamble Company
Food Products

Laundry Detergents
Personal-Care Products

The Quaker Oats Company
Pet-Food Products

*Ralston Purina Company
Food Products
Bread Products

*Richardson-Vicks Inc.
Skin Care Products
Hair Care Products

Rubbermaid, Inc.
Household Products

Schenley Industries
Alcoholic Beverages

*Schering Laboratories
Pharmaceuticals

*Joseph E. Seagram & Sons
Distilled Spirits

The Sheraton Corporation
Food and Beverage Services

Simon & Schuster
Book Publishing

The Southland Corporation
Convenience Stores

The Stanley Works
Hardware Products

Teledyne Water Pik
Home Appliances

Texas Instruments Incorporated
Electronics

Timex Corporation
Watches

Tupperware Home Parties
Housewares

UST Enterprises
Nontobacco Products

*The West Bend Company
Appliances

Repeat business is one indication of client satisfaction. An * indicates a corporation for which we have completed multiple assignments, or a subscriber to TrendPack.

Index

AARP (American Association of Retired Persons), 45, 57
Absolut vodka, 96–97
Acupressure and acupuncture, 67
Adams, John, 89
"Adrenaline Adjusting," 5–6
Adult Children of Alcoholics (ACoA), 46
Adult fun camps, 60
Advertising, future of, 165–66, 168–70
Aerosol sprays, 88
Agee, Mary Cunningham, 209
Aging. *See* Down-Aging
Ahrens, Ronald, 205–6
AIDS, 28, 29, 63, 85, 90, 97, 101, 162
Airlines, 31–32, 75–76, 137
Air pollution, 18
Alice in Wonderland, 78, 126
Alternative-energy plants, 89
Alzheimer's Disease, 58
American Express, 134
American Reforestry Association, 90
American spirit, 211
Amusement parks, 35
Androids, 188
Anheuser-Busch, 163
Answering machines, 29, 52, 80
Anti-depressant, 58
Anti-snooping devices, 29
Apfelbaum, Ben, 141

Aphrodisiacs, 36, 58
Apple Computer, 91, 185
Apples, Alar-treated, 70
Aroma business, 210–11
Aromatherapy, 5, 30, 67
Artificial reality, 109
AT&T, 90, 159
Audi, 75
Audio tapes, customized music for, 48
Automobiles, 97, 123–24, 136, 141, 183–85; Cocooning in, 30–31; customized features for, 47; electric, 88; "short-termism" in, 101–2
Ayurvedic medicine, 67

Bacardi Imports, 112–13
Bailey, Lee, 103
Barr, Roseanne, 22
Baum, Herbert M., 207
Beef, 65, 186
Belgian Shoes shop, 47
Ben & Jerry's, 87, 141
Benevolent and Loyal Order of Pessimists, 45
Benson, Diane, 103
Berra, Yogi, 183
Bicycles, custom-made, 47–48
Big Fun amusement parks, 181
Biodegradable bottles, 207
Biofeedback, 67

Bird-watching, 53
Birthrate, 28, 97
Blue Angel, 88
Bodyguards, 30, 180–81
Body Shop International (firm), 77, 87, 90
Bon Ami, 183
Booth, I. M., 204
Borden, 70
Boycotts, 72–73, 181
Brack, Reginald K., Jr., 204
Bradshaw, John, 55
Brain boosters, 58–59, 201
Brain gyms and clubs, 187
BrainReserve (marketing consulting firm), vii–
    viii, 7–8, 11; address of, 189; BrainJams at,
    102, 161; client list of, 215–20; consumer in-
    terviews by, 95, 148–52; Discontinuity
    Trends Analysis at, 104–13; methodology
    flow chart of, 213; reading list of, 198–200;
    TalentBank for, 12–13, 95, 102, 103; Trend-
    Packs of, 59–60, 102; TrendTracking at, 21–
    23, 95–103, 145–47; TrendView seminar at,
    100–1; Universal Screen Test at, 114–17
Brainstorming, 12–13
BrainWash (laundry/café), 83
Brands, 96, 183–85, 202, 203
Bread, marketing of, 8
Breatharians, 45
Bringers (firm), 82
Buatta, Mario, 28
"Bungee cord" jumpers, 74–75
Burger King, 181
Burke, Jim, 162
Burrowing, 180, 181
Bush, Barbara, 58
Buster Brown, 184
Butter, "fatter," 41

Cameras and film, 8, 127, 142
Campbell's, 160
Camping, 53, 185
Canada, 87, 88
Capitalists-for-decency, 86, 91–92
Carl's Jr. restaurant, 82
Carter, Jimmy, 90
Carter's, 184
Cashing Out, 7, 50–55, 107, 111, 113, 123, 135,
    154, 155, 211; to the country, 53–54; Vicari-
    ous, 54–55
Cause Marketing, 92
CBS, 71
Census, 6
Cereal boxes, 127
Chaos theory, 79
Charitable giving, 91
Chase Manhattan Bank, 90
Cheer, 88
Cher, 57
Chiat, Jay, 209
Chicken of the Sea, 74
Children, 174–76; environmental concerns
    of, 86, 174–76; as experts, 188; lost and
    found chips for, 188; Small Indulgences
    for, 41
Choel, Patrick, 210
Cholesterol, 66, 70
Christian Classic Bikers Association, 45
Chrysler, 183
Chung, Connie, 57
Clanning, 180
Clean Air Act, 89
Clean Water Act, 89
Cluster marketing, 83
CNN, 80

Coca-Cola, 90, 163; New Coke, fiasco of, 7, 74,
    98
Cocktail Hour at Home, 32–33
Cocooning, 7, 27–33, 106, 110, 112, 115, 117,
    119, 120, 141, 144, 145, 180; Armored, 29–
    30; Socialized, 32–33; Wandering, 30–32,
    141
Coffee, caffeine-free, 66
Coffey, Birch, 103
Colgate-Palmolive, 88
Collective living, 19
Collins, Joan, 57
Comedy Connection, 75
Community Capital Bank, 90
Community work, 19
Composting, 188
Computers: food ordered by, 82; as information
    editors, 84; mind-trips by, 187; for personal-
    ized fashion design, 47; personal relation-
    ships to deteriorate because of, 205; Virtual
    Reality through, 109–12; watchdog systems
    using, 20; and working at home, 52
Consume/replenish approach, 18
Consumers: databanks on, 143; moods of, vs.
    "types" of, 24–25; predicted sociacquake of,
    6–8, 19–20; pullback by, 133–35. See also
    Vigilante Consumer
ConsumerSpeak, 148–52
ConsumerTime, 153–55
Cornell University, 90
Corporate Soul, 159–63, 176
Corporations, 6, 18; basic values of, 203, 208;
    Cashing Out from, 7, 50–53, 55, 211; con-
    sumers' relationship with, 75–77, 143–44,
    159–63, 165, 176, 209; cultural autism in,
    21–22; early retirement in, 207–8; 800 num-
    bers of, 137–38; employees of, as target mar-
    kets, 202; employee volunteer programs of,
    91; environmental concerns of, 89–90, 160–
    63; future leadership of, 205; health of em-
    ployees of, 67; social responsibilities of, 19,
    91; work at home by employees of, 52–53,
    203
Cosmetics, 48, 67, 90, 142, 170, 173
Country inns, 53
Country Store, 141
Cream of Wheat, 184
Creativity, freedom necessary for, 11
Credit cards, 7, 133–35
Crime, 18, 19, 28, 29, 47
Culture, TrendTracking of, 21–26
Cuomo, Andrew, 89
Cuomo, Mario, 89
Cyberspace, 109

Dancers for Disarmament, 45
Dash, 88
Davis, Melinda, 81
Decency, 7, 86, 91–92, 160–61
Decession, 134
Dental care: at-home, 58; by fluoridated choco-
    late milk, 66; multi-functional approach to,
    83
Deprenyl, 58–59
Design Industries Foundation for AIDS
    (DIFFA), 162
Diana, Princess, 36
Diaz, Arnold, 71
Digestifs, 184
Discounting of high-ticket items, 42
Disease-dread, 63–64
Dishwashers, 82–83
Disneyland, 35, 82, 122
Disney World, 60

Dr. Seuss, 59
Dog food, healthier, 101
"Dolphin Safe" tunafish, 74
Donahue, Phil, 71
Dove Bar, 146
Down-Aging, 56–61, 87, 98, 107, 111, 113, 116, 154, 171–73
Downy, 88
Dream architects, 188
Drugs: crime and, 18, 19; food combined with, 5, 66, 184

Eco-settling, 187
Education, 5, 86, 91, 206
Education 1st!, 89–90
Egonomics, 43–49, 106–7, 110–11, 113, 115–16, 119, 122–24, 147, 180, 181
800 numbers, 137–38, 165, 176
Eisner, Eric, 89
Elston, Paul J., 89
Entrepreneurialism, 55, 211
Environment, 5, 85–92, 188, 210–11, 212; children and, 86; corporations and, 89–90, 160–63
Environmental Choice seal, 88
Era, 88
Espresso Dental, 83
Estée Lauder, 37, 135, 142
Ethics, 5, 86, 89–90, 208, 209, 212; female, in the marketplace, 188
Evans, John B., 45
Exercise Addiction, 63
Extremism approach, 121–24
Exxon, 72, 162

Families: changes in, 79; expanded, 187
Fantasy Adventure, 34–38, 106, 110, 113, 115, 116, 122, 123, 141, 146, 181
"Fanzines," 45
F.A.O. Schwarz, 60
Farmer, Carol, 100
Fashion: Egonomics as applied to, 46–47; Fantasy Adventure, 36–37
Fast food, 8, 82, 119, 121–22, 181; for babies, 188
Fatless fat, 66
Fax, 80–81, 82, 84, 136, 179
Fax Grande Cuisine (firm), 82
Federal Express, 136
Fiesta Mart (supermarket), 65
Fish farms, 65
Fitness/Fatness, 26
"Flash Fiction," 81
Flatow, Peter, 101
Flaum, Mechele, 10, 11, 59
Flaum, Sander A., 211
"Flextime," 52
Focus Groups, 149
Food: airline, 75–76; consumers' desire for fresh, 136; customized, 147; engineered-for-health, 65–66; exotic, 36, 146; grown under controlled conditions, 4–5, 65; nonviolence in, 186; organic, 65; poisons in, 63, 65; Small Indulgences in, 40–41; specialty, growth of business in, 40; speeding up of, 82–83; tracking trends in, 145–47; Twisting the Familiar in, 125–27; Vigilante Consumer and, 70–71
"Foodaceuticals," 5, 66, 184
Ford Motors, 124, 183
Forests, 90
Freedom, creativity and, 11
Friends of the Earth, 74
Fringe groups, 45
Fulghum, Robert, 55

Furness, Betty, 71
Future: Americans' positive attitude about, 210; business lessons of, 131–32; as collective effort, 12–13; history as means of knowing, 206; more diversity expected in, 204; packaging of, 99–103; of society, 85–86; two visions of, 17–20; various opinions on, 201–12. See also Trends

Gallo, Ernest & Julio, 90
Gallup Poll, 82
Gap, the, 141
Garbage, 17–18
Gardening, 53, 144
"Gardening clothes," 54
Garlanda, Gino, 100n.
Gays, as parents, 79
Genetic engineering, 65
General Foods, 135, 144
General Mills, 70, 82
General Motors, 88
Giant sizes, 126
Gillman, Richard, 206
Global Kids, 46, 174–76
"Goal Drinks," 66
Godiva Chocolates, 126, 160
Goeren, Cornelius J., 210–11
"Golden Oldies," 60
Good Housekeeping, 160–61
Grateful Dead, 57
Great Bear bottled water, 74
Green Cross, 88
Green Giant, 183
Greenhouse effect, 87, 90
Green Seal, 88
Gretzky, Wayne, 124
Gross, Amy, 103
Guarantees, 76–77, 143
Guber, Lynda, 89
Guess Jeans, 159
Gunn, Michael W., 202
Gun ownership, 29

Habitat for Humanity, 90
Haig & Haig Pinch, 184
Hair coloring, 57; customized, 48
Handcrafted products, 44
Hanft, Adam, 210
Hanks, Tom, 59
Harris Poll, 65
Hayward, Charlie, 146–47
Haza, Ofra, 37
HELP (organization), 89
Hempel, Amy, 81
Herbal treatments, 5
"Herb's Dump" (TV news segment), 71
Hertz, 80
"Hi Honey, I'm Home" (firm), 82
Holistic medicine, 67
Home: Cocooning at, 7, 29–30; customized equipment for, 48–49; as fortress, 4, 18–19, 29–30; as future shopping center, 164–67; greenhouses at, 204; working at, 30, 52
Home delivery, future of, 165
Homeless, the, 90
Homeopathy, 67
Home security systems, 29
Horowitz, David, 70–71
Hot-Branding, 140–42, 185
Hotels: "adventure" locales in, 35; rough, tough dude-ranch, 184
"Huddling and Cuddling," 32–33
Hyatt Hotels Corporation, 35
Hydroponic gardens, 65

IBM, 91, 135
Ice cream, 40
Ice cream cones, 125
Idaho potatoes, 73
In-Depth Interviews, 149
Indulging at Discount, 42
Information editors, 84
Institute for Consumer Responsibility, 72
Insurance: high cost of, 70; medical, 64
Internal Revenue Service (IRS), 124
International Resource Development, 81
Inventiveness, needed in American business, 211
Isenberg, Carole, 89, 211

Japan: aromatherapy in, 30; custom-made bicycles in, 47–48; Disneyland in, 35; over-extended economy of, 209; Preventive Business in, 136; skin research in, 58
Jefferson, Thomas, 19
Jobs, multiple, 79
Johnson & Johnson, 185, 203

Karan, Donna, 46
Kates, Henry E., 203
Keebler, 70
Keen, Sam, 208
Keillor, Garrison, 54
Kellogg (firm), 70
Kenmore, Ayse, 47
Kenmore, Bob, 47
Kleenex, 184
K mart, 91
Kodak, 74, 135, 162
Kovics, Stan, 12
Kraft (firm), 135, 144
Krause's Sofa Factory, 47
Kuralt, Charles, 55

Lang, k. d., 73, 186
Lanier, Jaron, 110
Latchkey kids, 46, 175
Lauder, Leonard A., 96, 183–85, 202, 203
Lauren, Ralph, 141
Lawsuits, helping poor in, 90
Lawyers, 123, 188
Leisure time, decrease of, 6
Leonard, Stew, 76
Levi's, 184
Licari, Louis, 48
Life stages, identity groups based on, 46
Light therapy, 5, 67–68, 186
Liquor, 66–67, 97, 112–13, 153, 184
Loblaw supermarket chain, 87–88
Long Lake Energy Corporation, 89
Lorelli, Michael K., 202
Lost and found chip, 188
Lyons, Chief Oren, 212

McDonald's, 74, 83, 125, 162, 184–85
McFarland, Brian, 207
McKeown, Jack, 147
MADD (Mothers Against Drunk Driving), 72–73
Madonna, 36
Magazines, 44–45, 87
Mail, future competition with U.S. Postal Service for, 204
Mailing envelopes, 127
Mail-order sales, 28, 164–65, 205; return policies on, 77; of X-rated products, 36
Management, participatory, 19
Manhattan Intelligence, 84
Marigold, Lys, 11, 47

Market fluctuations, 201–2, 204
Marketing, 8; Cause, 92; cluster, 83; cross-, 144; moral transformation through, 86; time lag in, 153–55
Market niches, 76, 180
Marram, Ellen, 204
Martin, Ian A., 201
Mason, Jackie, 60
Matsushita (firm), 47–48
Mattress tags, 75
Mazda Miata, 141
Medicine, 64–65, 67–68, 123, 188
Merck, 184
Merlo, Ellen, 205
Microwave oven, 82, 143–44
Miles One-a-Day Vitamins, 184
Miller Brewing, 144, 163
Miniature sizes, 126
Mood Food, 66
MovieFone, 84
Movies: of adults and kids switching bodies, 59; erotic, 36; over-40 audience for, 60; Scent-a-Rama, 37
Multi-function, 83
Murdoch, Rupert, 45
Music: customized, for audio tapes, 48; Fantasy Adventure, 37; in "The Me Decade," 43
Myer, Sandra, 208–9

Nabisco, 125
Nader, Ralph, 70, 169
National parks, theater tours of, 37
National Resources Defense Council, 70, 89
Natural law, 212
Nayad, 58
Neighborhood office center, 52–53
Nelson, Paul, 112
Nepal, 90
Nestlé company, 72
Networking, 18
New Age Arrogance, 57–59
Newbold, Joanne, 103
Newfield, Bert, 12
Newman, Paul, 57
Newspapers, 44, 87
New York Marathon, 57
Nike sports shoes, 141
Nikon, 141
Nimodopine, 58
900 numbers, 138, 144
99 Lives, 78–84, 108, 111, 113, 116–17, 119, 122–24, 154, 179
Nintendo, 60, 110, 175, 187
Nissan, 103
Nonviolence, 186
Nostalgia, 60, 146, 210
Nuclear weapons, 89, 175
NutraSweet, 66
Nutrition advisers of service companies, 66

Offices, future services in, 83
Olestra, 66
Onassis, Jacqueline, 56
Opel, John R., 205
Oreo cookies, 146
Osgood, Charles, 55
Out-of-body meetings, 45
Outward Bound, 90
Overeaters Anonymous (OA), 46
Ozbek, Rifat, 36

Paccione, Onofrio, 12
Packaging, 126–27, 165, 207, 210–11
Pajamas, 28

INDEX

Palermo, Peter M., 208
Pan Am, 75
Panasonic bicycles, 47–48
Paper, substitute for, 90
Paper towels, 88
Paris (France), 82
Patagonia (firm), 77, 87, 176
Pathfinder, 184
Patriotism, 182
Pazzani, Martin J., 205
People for the Ethical Treatment of Animals, 73
Pepperidge Farm, 70, 127, 160
Pepsi-Cola, 163
Perdue, Frank P., 185, 209
Perfume, 101
Perkins, Brian D., 203
Perrier water, 74, 96, 138
Persian Gulf War, 80, 181, 182
Personics (firm), 48
Pesticides, 65, 72, 127
Peters, Jon, 89
Peterson, Peter G., 207
Pets: care of, 84; owning of, 28
Philip Morris, 135, 144
Phillips, Robert M., 201–2
Phoenix House, 89
Phone chat lines, 28, 36
Photoplex (sunscreen), 58
Piedra, Freddie, 112
Pietersen, William G., 203
Pillsbury, 70
Pittman, Stuart, 12, 169
Pizza Anytime machine, 82
Pleasure trips, length of, 40
Politics: future of, 206; lack of ethics in, 5
Polykoff, Shirley, 12
Popcorn, origin of name, 100n.
Porizkova, Paulina, 37
Press Box News, 83
Preventive Business, 133–36
Procter & Gamble, 66, 88, 163
Psychoenergizer, 58
Public school system, 205
Purina, 101
Putnam, Todd, 72

Quaker Oats, 67, 70
Quality of life, infrastructure and, 208–9

Rakolta, Terry, 70
Ralston Purina, 70
Rawl, Lawrence G., 162
Recessions, 5, 134
Recreation, money spent on, 60
Recycling, 13, 74, 88–89, 92, 161–63
Red Dye No. 2, 72
Reebok, 74–75, 97
Reflexology, 67
Religion: cult, 45; return to, 54, 97
Restaurants, 28, 98, 146; ice cream cafés, 40
Retin-A, 57
Return policies, 77
Revlon, 36
Reynolds, R. J. (firm), 75
Rice, C. Duncan, 206
Riese, Phillip J., 206
Roddick, Anita, 77, 90, 202
Rogers, Peter N., 207–8
Rolling Stones, 57
Rosenthal, Mitch, 89
Roto-Rooter, 84
Roux, Michel, 204

Rubbermaid, 90, 161–62
Rubin, Harriet, 14

Sabbatical leave, 187
Salt, cutting down on, 97
Santelli, Tony, 135
Sardina, Eddie, 112
Schmitt, Wolf, 161
Schumacher, Joel, 89
Schwinn, 184
Scott, Willard, 55
Scuba diving, 35–36
Seagram's, 163
Searchers, 45
Security screens, 188
Self-health care, 64–65, 67
Sexual adventures, 36
"Shame on You" (TV news segment), 71
Shampoo, 127
Shane, Ted, 12
Shanghai (China), 9
Sharper Image, The (store), 60
Shiseido, 58
Shoes, 47, 141, 185
Shopping, future of, 35, 164–67, 202, 205–6, 208
Shorin, Arthur T., 212
Shower Massage, The, 118–19
Siegel, Ronald K., 67
Sierra Club, 70
Simon, Paul, 37
Simon & Schuster, 146–47
Simplesse, 66
Single parents, 79
Sixth Street Marketplace, 84
Skadden, Arps, Slate, Meagher & Flom, 90
Skin-care market, 58
Slow Food Foundation, The, 54
Small Indulgences, 39–42, 106, 110, 113, 115, 116, 122, 123, 141, 146, 180, 210
Smith, Marty, 169
Smith & Hawken, 54
Smith-Greenland Advertising, 12
Social Security, 61
Social work, graduate schools of, 91
Sofas, custom-designed, 47
Sokoloff, Phil, 70
Solow, Martin, 12
Sony, 175
S.O.S. (Save Our Society), 85–92, 108–9, 111, 113, 123, 124
Soup, canned, 136
Special interest groups, 45–46
Specialty boutiques, future of, 166
Speed of technology, 80
Speed service, 83–84
Stanley Tools, 119–20
Star-Kist, 74
Staying Alive, 62–68, 107, 111, 113, 116, 119, 122, 136, 153
Steinem, Gloria, 173
Stengel, Casey, 15
Stewart, Martha, 103, 208
Streamlining, 81–83
Streep, Meryl, 70
Stress, 25, 29, 34, 40, 51, 59, 81, 116, 201
Stress Man, 67
Stuffed animals, 41
Sunbeam, 67
Sunshine Biscuits, 70
Supermarkets, 65, 87–88, 188; Discontinuity Trend Analysis of, 105–13
Surgery, plastic and reconstructive, 57, 187

INDEX

Survivor Kids, 85
Swissair, 75

Take-out food, 82
Tartikoff, Brandon, 89
Taylor, Elizabeth, 57
Teddy bears, shampoo for, 41
Teledyne, 119
Telephones, 80
Television: children's environmental shows on, 86; consumer advocates on, 70–71; folksy nice guys on, 55; protests against shows on, 70; trends in shows on, 22; viewer loyalty on, 45
Theme parks, 35
Tide, 88
Time: transformation of, 80–82. *See also* ConsumerTime
Time Warner, Inc., 71, 135
Timex, 184
Tom's of Maine, 87
Tool kit, 119–20
Touch 2000 machine, 82
Toxic Substances Control Act, 89
Toyota, 136
Toys, dangerous, 72
Travel for health and longevity, 67
TrendBending, 118–20
TrendPacks, 59–60, 102
Trends: average length of, 25, 154; Brain-Reserve's tracking of, 21–23, 95–103, 145–47; consumer moods tapped into by, 24–26; contradictory, 25–26; Discontinuity Trends Analysis, 104–13; signals for, 179–82; Universal Screen Test for, 114–17. *See also specific trends: Cashing Out; Cocooning; Down-Aging; Egonomics; Fantasy Adventure; 99 Lives; Small Indulgences; S.O.S.; Staying Alive; Vigilante Consumer*
Triads (research groups of consumers), 149
Trillin, Calvin, 54
Tropical oils, 70

Tupperware, 184
Twain, Mark, 55
Twisting the Familiar, 125–27
Tylenol, 73–74, 162

Uniformity, change in attitude toward, 44
Universal Screen Test, 114–17

VCRs, 28; pre-programming of, 48; taping by, 81
Video rentals, erotic, 36
VideoTown Laundrette, 83
Vigilante Consumer, 69–77, 92, 107–8, 111, 113, 141, 175, 181
Virtual Reality, 109–12
Visich de Visoko, Marquis, 211
Vitamins, 184
Vitamin tonics, 66
Volunteerism, 90–91
Volvo, 75

Waldenbooks, 115–16
Wal-Mart stores, 88
Walters, Barbara, 74
Water pollution, 63, 65, 181
Weather, customized, 49
Week-at-a-Glance calendar, 81
Welcome Wagon, 144
West, Dick, 212
West, Needham, 119
Wexner, Leslie H., 210
Whitman's chocolates, 185
Williams, Diane, 81
Winfrey, Oprah, 22, 71
Women Who Love Too Much, 46
Wurman, R. S., 80

Xerox, 91

"Youth Culture," 98

Ziskin, Laura, 89